Aloha to Nancy

Katharine Luomala

HULA KI'I
HAWAIIAN PUPPETRY

Hula Ki'i, oil on canvas by Jean Charlot, 1971.
Henry Blakstad Collection.

HULA KI'I
HAWAIIAN PUPPETRY

Katharine Luomala

published by
The Institute for Polynesian Studies
funded by the
Polynesian Cultural Center
Brigham Young University—Hawaii Campus

Hula Ki'i: Hawaiian Puppetry

published by The Institute for Polynesian Studies
funded by the Polynesian Cultural Center
Brigham Young University—Hawaii Campus

Copyright © 1984 The Institute for Polynesian Studies

All Rights Reserved
Manufactured in the United States of America

Distributed for The Institute for Polynesian Studies
by the University of Hawaii Press:

Order Department
University of Hawaii Press
2840 Kolowalu Street
Honolulu, Hawaii 96822

ISBN 0-939154-30-7

Book design by Judi Thompson

CONTENTS

Illustrations, vii
Preface, xi
Introduction, 1

Part I.   Description of Museum Puppet Figures and Heads, 13

    A.   Puppet Figures, 15
        1.   Introduction, 15
        2.   British Museum Puppet, 17
        3.   Nine Puppets in American Museums, 24
            a.   Introduction, 24
            b.   Six National Museum Puppets, 25
            c.   Three Bishop Museum Puppets, 33

    B.   Two Aberrant Bishop Museum Images, 51
        1.   Introduction, 51
        2.   The "Doll," 51
        3.   The "Puppet," 52

    C.   A Torso and Separate Puppet Heads in Museums, 55
        1.   Introduction, 55
        2.   Berlin Museum Torso, 55
        3.   British Museum Head (Haw. 77), 58
        4.   British Museum Head (Haw. 76), 60
        5.   The Missing Head, 61
        6.   Berlin Museum Head, 64

Part II.   Functions and Kinds of *Hula Ki'i,* 69

    A.   Functions, 71

    B.   Kinds of *Hula Ki'i,* 79
        1.   Introduction, 79
        2.   Theatrics, 79

HULA KI'I: Hawaiian Puppetry

- C. *Hula Ki'i* with a Screen, 85
    1. Puppets as Dancers, 85
    2. Puppet Plays, 91
    3. Human Participation in Puppetry Acts, 97
        a. Entr'actes, 97
        b. Dancers, 99
- D. *Hula Ki'i* without a Screen, 117
    1. Imitations of Puppets Dancing; No Puppets Present, 117
        a. The 1780s and 1820s; Kamakau and Kepelino, 117
        b. 1883, Kalākaua's Coronation, 122
        c. Four Other Nineteenth-century *Hula Ki'i*, 126
    2. Human Imitations of Sacred Images, Present or Absent, 131
    3. Puppets as Human Dancers' Body Masks, 135
    4. Puppet Actors with Human Dancers, 136

Part III. Narratives about Magical and Legendary Images Imitating People, 139

- A. Introduction, 141
- B. The Heroes and Heroines of the Narratives, 143
    1. Kaipalaoa, 143
    2. Halemano, 144
    3. Kauakāhiakawa'ū, 146
    4. Konikonia, 148
    5. Wākea, 150
    6. Māui, 152
    7. Pūpūhulu'ana, 163
    8. Kau'ilani, 163
    9. Kawelo, 164
    10. Pi'imaiwa'a, 164
    11. Kaneopa, 165
    12. Hi'iaka, 166
    13. Hoamakeikekula, 166

Summary, 169
Bibliography, 173
Index, 179

ILLUSTRATIONS

Frontispiece *Hula Ki'i,* oil on canvas by Jean Charlot, 1971. Henry Blakstad Collection.

PART I

1. Old California playbill, circa 1850s. (Hawaii State Archives), 43.
2. *A Man of the Sandwich Islands, Dancing.* (Louis Choris, 1816), 44.
3. *Ahu'ena Heiau, Hawaii.* (Choris), 45.
4. *An Offering before Capt. Cook in The Sandwich Islands.* (John Webber, 1778), 45.
5. "Idol." British Museum puppet with tapa skirt. (J. G. Wood sketch, 1877), 46.
6. Disassembled British Museum puppet. (Ben Burt photos), 46.
7. The assembled British Museum puppet, 47.
8–9. Kini Ki'i or "King Image." National Museum of Natural History, Smithsonian Institution. (Martha Cooper photos), 48.
10–11. Puapuakea or "White Cock's Tail Feathers," 48.
12–13. Mailelauli'i or "Small-leafed Maile," 49.
14–15. Mailepākaha or "Blunt-leafed Maile," 49.
16–17. Makakūikalani or "Royal Boaster," 50.
18–19. Nihiaumoe or "Midnight Prowler," 50.

PART II

20. Pa'akaula and his puppets at Bishop Museum. (Bernice P. Bishop Museum photo), 103.
21. Pa'akaula's puppets, close up. (George Bacon photos), 104.
22. Mākālei or "Magical Fish Stick" in profile, 104.
23. Frontal view of Mākālei's T-shaped torso and hinged arms, 104.
24. Clothed Mākālei, 104.
25. Pa'akaula's puppets, dressed, 105.
26. Puppet family performs at Bishop Museum behind a tapa screen. (Bernice P. Bishop Museum photo), 105.

HULA KI'I: Hawaiian Puppetry

27. "Punch and Judy," by George Cruikshank, 1828. (Böhmer, 1971), 106.
28. "Punch on his travels," by George Cruikshank. (J. P. Collier, 1828), 106.
29. "Mr. Punch." (Collier), 107.
30–31. British Museum head no. "Haw. 76." (Ben Burt photos), 108.
32. Berlin Museum für Völkerkunde head. (Dr. Gerd Koch photo), 109.
33. Berlin Museum für Völkerkunde torso. (Dr. Gerd Koch photo), 110.
34. Sketches painted by Sarah Stone. Upper left sketch illustrates British Museum head "Haw. 77." (Force and Force, 1968), 111.
35. Bishop Museum articulated "doll." (Bernice P. Bishop Museum photo), 112.
36. Bishop Museum unarticulated "puppet." (Bernice P. Bishop Museum photo), 113.
37–38. British Museum head no. "Haw. 77." (Ben Burt photo), 114.
39. Queen Ka'ahumanu by Louis Choris. (Bernice P. Bishop Museum photo), 115.
40. "Feather idol." (John Webber, 1778), 116.

PART III

41. Kamehameha The Great (Bernice P. Bishop Museum photos), 153.
42. Kamehameha II (Liholiho), 154.
43. Kamehameha III (Kauikeaoūli), 154.
44. Portrait of Nāhi'ena'ena by Robert Dampier, 1825. (Honolulu Academy of Arts photos), 155.
45. Kamehameha III, companion portrait by Dampier, 155.
46. Kamehameha IV (Alexander Liholiho), (Bernice P. Bishop Museum photos), 156.
47. Kamehameha V (Lot), 156.
48. William Charles Lunalilo, 156.
49. Kalākaua (David Kalākaua), 157.
50. Lili'uokalani (Lydia Paki), 158.
51. King Kalākaua Coronation, 1883. (Bernice P. Bishop Museum photos), 159.
52. Dandy Ioane and Hula Girls, 159.

Illustrations

53. Winona Beamer Hula Troupe performing *hula ki'i* at Moanalua Gardens, Prince Lot Hula Festival, Honolulu, 1978. (Winona Beamer photos), 160.
54. Winona Beamer and dancers perform *hula ki'i*, 160.
55. Modern puppet stage at the festival, 161.
56. Women dancers wearing body masks perform *hula ki'i*, 161.
57. Boy dancers with hand puppets at the festival, 161.
58. Iolani Luahine in *hula ki'i* pose: The Dance of the Graven Images. (G. P. Noble photo, *Paradise of the Pacific* 58:38, 1946), 162.
59. Mary Pukui and her daughter, Pele. (Martha Homsey photo, *Paradise of the Pacific* 58:39, 1946), 162.

PREFACE

Grateful acknowledgment is due the National Science Foundation and the Smithsonian Institution for making it possible for me in 1966, as Visiting Senior Research Fellow, to study Pacific collections at the National Museum of Natural History, Smithsonian Institution, Washington, D.C. Were it not for them I should never have strayed into such a happy bypath as that lined with Hawaiian puppets as well as images, masks, and puppets from elsewhere in Polynesia. My thanks also go to the staff at the National Museum, and at the British Museum, Berlin Museum für Völkerkunde, Hawaii State Archives, Honolulu Academy of Arts, and Bernice P. Bishop Museum for their patient and generous assistance. I appreciate the permission from Moanalua Gardens Foundation, Inc. to quote from Mrs. Gertrude MacKinnon Damon's notebooks. I also wish to thank Winona Beamer and Samuel H. Elbert for their considerable contributions to this study of *hula ki'i*. I also wish to thank Henry Blakstad and the family of the late Jean Charlot for permission to reproduce Charlot's interpretations of *hula ki'i*. At the British Museum, Ben Burt photographed several *ki'i* for me as did Martha Cooper at the National Museum. And at The Institute for Polynesian Studies, editors Gloria Cronin and Judi Thompson did all they could to assemble the illustrations and comb out my mistakes. Any that remain are my fault and not those of all who helped me.

Katharine Luomala

INTRODUCTION

This three-part study centers on the description, function, and conjectural history of Hawaiian puppetry. Serendipity led me to investigate Polynesian puppetry and masking after I happened to pull out the wrong drawer at the National Museum of Natural History, Washington, D.C. in 1966 (Luomala 1973, 1978, 1979, 1981), and saw the six royal Hawaiian puppets described by N. B. Emerson in *Unwritten Literature of Hawaii* (1909:91–102, Plates VIII, IX). It was like seeing friends alive I had thought long since "hid in death's dateless night" although I had never seen them before except in Emerson's book. In Part I, I shall describe in detail the existing puppets in museums, and in Part II, what is known about the functions and kinds of puppet performance (*hula ki'i*, image dance) now nearly extinct except for recent revivals in modified form. Part III tells about narratives in which images magically imitate people.

Most of what is known today is based on a few ambiguous, generalized references, some eyewitness accounts and some wooden, humanoid images in museums—ten legless, manipulable hand puppets; three detached heads; and two legless images and a torso some scholars think were used in puppetry. The first eyewitness description of a puppetry performance was from Kaua'i in 1820, forty-two years after Captain Cook's arrival there. King Kaumuali'i and Queen Kapule, rulers of Kaua'i, hosts in earlier years to English and Russian voyagers, now sought to amuse two newly arrived American Protestant missionary couples with a puppet dance. Six undescribed puppets danced a hula. They rose from behind a tapa screen stretched across the room in front of the audience and the musician seated on the floor. The puppets timed their motions to the beat by an old man who drummed and sang. Judging the exhibition "folly & vanity," the guests left early (E. Damon 1925:208).

Today there are very few Hawaiian puppeteers but they retain elements of this basic pattern while supplementing it with innovations, some inspired by Western forms. This kind of artistic interaction, like the history of foreign theaters and the rest of foreign culture introduced into the islands, is relevant to the problem of whether Hawaiians had puppetry when Cook arrived in 1778. In the early historic era, local entertainers in port towns soon modified their performances to adapt them to foreign audiences. Likewise foreign entertainers, residents or visitors, added local features to their acts.

The earliest reference to a foreign theater and play illustrates the point (Campbell 1822:148–149;Hoyt 1961:8–9). Archibald Campbell, a disabled Scottish seaman who spent about thirteen months during 1809 and 1810 in Honolulu under Kamehameha's protection, saw a performance of "Oscar and Malvina," a drama based on Ossian's poems, at a theater built under the direction of James Beattie, Kamehameha's block-maker for ships' rigging and a former actor in England. Beattie had composed a few lines in English for his Hawaiian cast. To portray scenes of a Scottish castle and forest, he pasted together pieces of colored tapa and fashioned Highland garb of tapa for the Hawaiian men who played warriors and carried muskets. The role of Malvina, who escaped from her abductors and returned to Oscar, her fiance, was played by a chiefess, wife of Isaac Davis, one of Kamehameha's foreign advisors. (Whether she was Kaloakea or his second wife, Kalukuna [Grace Kamaikui], is not reported.) She won much applause although her lines were limited to "Yes" and "No." Unreported is whether Kamehameha was present or assisted behind scenes as he did in 1794 for an open-air four-act hula program to entertain Vancouver. According to Campbell, spectators (probably mostly Hawaiian for fewer than sixty whites were on the island) found Beattie's play hard to follow but enjoyed the afterpiece in which an overly realistic representation of a naval battle nearly burned down the theater.

Although islanders had already met numerous foreigners during the four decades between Cook's visit and the Kaua'i puppet show, nothing points to foreign introduction of puppets. By 1798 there had been visits, some more than once, by eight British expeditions, including Cook's, and two French expeditions. Between 1803 and 1826, there had been six Russian expeditions,

Introduction

two French, three British, and one American (Buck 1953). Hawaiian nobility soon had storehouses filled with those articles, either purchased or received as gifts, that they had not put immediately to use. So quickly were selected material and psychological changes integrated into the culture that it is now often difficult to tell without documentation what is foreign and what is native. However, commanders of visiting ships list no puppets among official gifts they presented to chiefs and chiefesses, or they received from them. Ships' officers officially entertained islanders with displays of fireworks, and sailors unofficially entertained the residents. Islanders, in turn, demonstrated their sports, games, and hula. (Hoyt 1961;Barrère 1980:15–26.) Before the end of the eighteenth century, Hawaiians were travelling to many parts of the world on foreign ships, which often took them on board as live "savage curiosities" to exhibit at home. Records about those travellers who finally got back to the islands do not mention puppets among the novelties they brought from abroad.

In 1830, marionettes as a gift from foreigners are mentioned for the first and only time—none too reliably, in my opinion—by Post Captain Otto von Kotzebue on his second major Pacific expedition. His six-day stay in Honolulu in 1825 was two months after the departure to England of HMS *Blonde,* commanded by Captain the Right Honourable Lord (George Anson) Byron, the poet's cousin. It had brought to the islands the bodies of King Kamehameha II (Liholiho) and Queen Kamāmalu, who had died in London.

Von Kotzebue (1830,II:143) states: *"Lord Byron hatte aus England allerlei Spielwerk mitgebracht, Marionetten, Schattenspiel u. vgl. um den Insulaner vergnügen zu machen"* (Lord Byron had brought with him from England various toys—marionettes, magic lanterns, and the like—in order to give pleasure to the islanders). Von Kotzebue mentions Byron's toys only because he heard of the contretemps and brouhaha over the unintentional error in scheduling an exhibition of the "phantasms" of the magic lantern (there was, it seems, only one) on the same night as high-ranking converts customarily held prayer meeting. Of the several writers who describe the embarrassing mixup, only von Kotzebue states that Byron had brought marionettes as well as a "phantasmagoria."

The popularity of marionettes and magic lanterns in Europe during this era may have led von Kotzebue to add marionettes among the toys he would expect Byron to bring. Had there really been any marionettes, their novelty would have been principally in their foreign appearance and mode of operation since some Hawaiians like Kaumuali'i already had hand puppets. However, no reference occurs to a marionette show enroute to the islands or after arrival. On the other hand, a magic lantern show entertained the surviving members of the royal entourage on the return voyage during festivities for crossing the Equator; and on shore, the show was put on in both Honolulu and Hilo in addition to the usual fireworks. Byron promised to give the phantasmagoria when he left to Prime Minister Kalanimoku who was particularly interested in the mechanics of its operation. (A. Bloxam 1925:10,48,55;R. R. Bloxam 1923:70;Byron 1826:146–150.)

By the 1850s, Honolulu, a growing port town, had begun to build commercial theaters in which entertainers on Pacific or world tours performed in variety shows, concerts, operas, and plays and augmented their casts with Hawaiian and local foreign talent. The foreign puppets, marionettes, automata, waxworks, and wooden black-faced minstrels in variety shows helped, as I shall discuss in Part II, to keep alive native puppetry, which, like all hula, the missionaries and their converts were trying to wipe out as "folly & vanity." The variety shows and the native puppetry of that era appealed to spectators of every age and rank, unlike the twentieth-century puppetry that is locally performed mainly for children and eliminates the ribaldry characteristic of the past.

The archipelago also exported its own art. A playbill of the 1850s from California gives the program of entrepreneur Charles Derby's travelling Hawaiian hula troupe. For fifty cents, men ("Ladies Prohibited") could see it (Archives of Hawaii; Scott 1968: 83). The next to the last feature listed is "Hula Kii, or the Dance of the Puppets" by the two girls in the troupe who presumably imitated puppets doing a hula while their five male colleagues sang and drummed for them.

Introduction

Native puppetry encompasses not only inanimate, manipulable images but human dancers who imitate them. Because Hawaiians call the total art *hula ki'i* whether done by live or wooden performers, and writers rarely state which kind they mean, one must guess what it is from the context.

A *ki'i* is any humanoid image, wooden or stone, sacred or secular, including a puppet. Many nineteenth-century writers applied the terms "idol" and "temple image" indiscriminately to any "artificial curiosity" they obtained from people different from themselves. As a result, it is often difficult to determine the function of any undocumented image they mention. Fortunately, Kaumuali'i's missionary guests who called his puppets "idols" explained their use in entertainment and thus made clear that, in the usage of the time, an idol was any native representation, not necessarily sacred.

To become sacred, a Hawaiian image must be ritually consecrated. Then it becomes a material symbol of a supernatural being whose spirit may enter it to receive offerings and prayers and perhaps transmit messages for its guardian to interpret. Until then the object is non-sacred. In the past many secular images had a decorative function in front of a chief's house or an important heiau. These images were usually less well made than those inside the stone or wooden-palisaded walls of a heiau (Kamakau 1961:202–203;1976:136). Because religion permeated the entire culture, these images, like those to be consecrated, were made by sculptors *(kāhuna kālai ki'i)* under ritual conditions directed by a master specialist of chiefly rank whose training in the proper rites, prayers, and lore made him a priest. For a heiau (an open-air temple complex with various structures), the secular images stood on that part of the stone pavement which was outside the walls enclosing the sacred, tabooed precincts. Another function of these ornamental figures may have been to warn passers-by of the sanctity of the area. Such a reminder, I think, was probably unnecessary before the abandonment of the native religion in 1819.

Referring to such figures and certain others associated with a heiau as secondary or auxiliary images, Cox and Davenport

HULA KI'I: Hawaiian Puppetry

(1974:59–61) suggest that although they "were not the central focus of the ceremonies . . . they were not merely decorative or a proliferation of the major image" in the tabooed area. "Each one," the writers add, "would have been known by a specific name, and each probably had some particular part to play in the temple ceremonies or demarcated specific ritual space." However, as noted above, S. M. Kamakau, a Hawaiian scholar, specifically refers to the images placed outside the walled area as having a decorative function.

The auxiliary images are especially relevant in the study of Hawaiian puppetry because of the puppet-like arm positions of two humanoid images depicted standing outside the walled area of 'Ahu'ena Heiau, Kailua, Hawai'i, by Louis Choris (1822:Plate V) in 1816 during von Kotzebue's first expedition as commander. No other artist has sketched similar figures, and museums have no examples. Kamehameha the Great in the early 1800s having conquered the islands restored and rededicated the heiau. Formerly dedicated to his war god, it was then dedicated to Lono, god of peace, fertility, and prosperity. It was one of many restored by Kamehameha, a very religious man. He often spent evenings at 'Ahu'ena with his council of chiefs while he instructed Liholiho, his chosen successor, in the traditions and proper behavior necessary to a ruler (I'i 1959:129).

The two images, along with two others, stand on the unwalled extension of the stone platform, and were probably assembled from separate parts and given movable arms like Hawaiian puppets. Drapery from the neck down, however, conceals their construction and even whether they were legless like the puppets. Each seems to be supported on a single post. That the two images belong to the same tradition as the puppets assembled from parts is suggested by their flexible-looking, tubular, widely extended arms and widespread fingers. The upraised arms contrast with the immovable pendant arms of most heiau images. One wonders if the two images' arms were adjustable. Each image appears to be enveloped in a short, rectangular tapa mantle *(kīhei)*, such as either sex wore as protection against the weather. Usually the upper border was thrown over the left shoulder and the two ends

Introduction

knotted at the right. The third figure on the platform, also apparently on a post, has a realistic looking human head and oddly placed, stumpy, fingerless, pendant arms. Instead of a mantle it has what look like short trousers hanging from its waist. There are no legs or feet visible. The fourth figure, supported on two tall thin poles, looks like a bundle of vegetation marked with a humanoid face. A very crudely carved wooden figure with upraised arms is in the Munich Ethnological Museum (Brigham 1913:283;284, Fig. 216). It vaguely resembles other figures with bent knees. The arms are tapered in a way to prevent their ever having been a support for an object.

The upraised arms of the three images call to mind a rite performed during a ten-day ceremony in Papa'ena'ena Heiau, Honolulu. It was one of the most sacred type *(luakini)* in which human beings were sacrificed. In this rite held inside the tabooed area, men, sitting cross-legged, were told to "put up the hands, up above." They then raised one or both hands with the right thumb erect. Anyone able to maintain this position during the hour-long prayers later boasted that he did not move even when a rat or a lizard crawled over him (I'i 1959:44).

Choris's sketch not only predates Kaumuali'i's *hula ki'i* show but the destruction in 1819 of numerous religious objects and structures when Liholiho, on becoming king, agreed with his closest advisors to give the death blow to the Hawaiian religion and the taboo system on which it rested. He publicly violated a major interdiction—that against men eating with women and eating food cooked in the same earth oven as theirs. The significance of "free eating," a denial of the power of the gods and of their earthly descendants, the nobility, to punish taboo violations, led people of every social class to follow the high priest's example by burning religious artifacts and structures. However, opponents faithful to the gods hid their images and secretly made new ones. In 1820, Kaumuali'i told his missionary guests that he had burned most of his images because "his gods had always fooled him and were good for nothing." Of a few he had "reserved for curiosity," he gave his guests two of his "favorite idols," which they sent to Boston to two members of the mission board. (Damon 1925:206,

HULA KI'I: Hawaiian Puppetry

210.) Nothing indicates that the two undescribed images came from his puppet troupe, the fate of which is unknown.

The "free eaters" probably destroyed anything called a *ki'i*, whether sacred or secular. Years before she became a Christian, Dowager Queen Ka'ahumanu, one of Kamehameha the Great's widows and a leader in the 1819 revolution, became the most zealous of all image-burners. Strong-willed and politically powerful, she was Liholiho's regent and foster mother. In 1822, while touring Hawai'i with Kaumuali'i (whom she had taken from Kapule to become one of her husbands), she searched out and burned over a hundred images (Bingham 1847:162). Three years later as a Protestant convert, she burned more, for they were still being made and worshipped. She also tried to stamp out kahuna-ism (Kamakau 1961:323). In her zeal to eliminate all "idol worship" *(malama ki'i* or *ho'omana ki'i)* she also took from the few Catholic converts of the time "their little *kii* (images of the cross, etc.)" (Bingham 1847:373; Kamakau 1961:329).

The very words *ki'i* and *hula ki'i* therefore boded ill for native puppetry, other types of hulas, songs, and anything else considered heathenism and a waste of time. As time went on, a puppeteer-hula master perhaps risked accusations of being either a *kahuna ki'i,* a priestly caretaker of heiau images (formerly an important position) or a kahuna dealing in evil sorcery. The term kahuna (for an expert in some facet of culture, a person carefully trained in the spiritual and material aspects of an occupation or profession) became in the Christian era an opprobrious term for a person suspected of practicing black magic, witchcraft, fetishism, and rites of the old religion. After her conversion, Ka'ahumanu, outdoing the missionaries in narrow interpretation of her new religion, sought to convert everyone and to bring order to a kingdom disorganized by both foreign influences and the abrogation of traditional taboos. She promulgated oral laws—"innumerable laws, laws upon laws"—enforced by her still fearful personal taboo, political power, and severe punishments (Kamakau 1961:288, 298–299). Hula and its songs were forbidden, but nonetheless were defiantly continued, especially in Honolulu, to entertain foreign seamen and to get an income. Only remote rural areas less

Introduction

affected by Western ways maintained hula and other pastimes as an integral part of traditional life.

With so much Hawaiian art destroyed, only museum material including the puppets can provide information about wooden images of the human figure. (See two definitive studies: *Arts and Crafts of Hawaii* by Peter H. Buck [1957:467–495] and *Hawaiian Sculpture* by J. Halley Cox and William H. Davenport [1974].) Buck is primarily concerned with specific "traditional" (pre-1819) techniques and structural form rather than function. He ignores all those images used for *hula ki'i* despite their many similarities to traditional sculpture. He also ignores their occasional exemplifications of previously unreported techniques. Cox and Davenport (1974:28,29,192–193), who are also concerned only with what they consider traditional wooden sculpture, nonetheless include one puppet figure and three separate heads in their survey of approximately one hundred and fifty examples left from the half-century after first Western contact. They classify these artifacts as to functional types and specialized forms. My survey incorporates all carved figures in museums that may have been connected with *hula ki'i* in any period through the early twentieth century.

Because of the 1819 bonfires and the perishable nature of wood (the major material for images) Cox and Davenport (pp. 23–24) think it "unlikely that any of the Hawaiian sculpture existing today was produced before A.D. 1750," but assume that the existing pieces "are a reasonably typical sampling of those that existed just prior to the overthrow of the old religion." To reconstruct and analyze the sculptural tradition of this fifty-year span, they further assume "that the variation in style among all of the types, except for a few that exhibit European influences, is not due to historical change but represents the variation within the tradition at the period just prior to the overthrow of the old religion." They also point out that "the age of any of the existing examples is almost impossible to determine." For these two authors, as for Buck, 1819 marks the end of the Hawaiian sculptural tradition.

To supplement relevant data from these two important studies, it is useful to consider the puppets within the framework of the

HULA KI'I: Hawaiian Puppetry

four categories of indigenous Polynesian art suggested by A. L. Kaeppler (1978:40-41;1979:185-186). "Traditional art" covers objects "produced at the time of first European contact." The second category, "evolved traditional art," continues and evolves "along indigenous lines retaining its traditional basic structure and sentiment," but is made perhaps with metal tools, similar but introduced raw materials, and an occasional European design element. The third category, "folk art," "the living art of the community," is produced perhaps with dissimilar materials, great structural changes, and "a creative combination of traditional and nontraditional concepts and values." The fourth category, "airport or tourist art," is produced with or without traditional precedents and is principally for sale to non-Hawaiians who often use it without knowledge of Hawaiian culture.

These categories, while not entirely chronological and often requiring subjective assessment of intangibles like sentiment and values, indicate that Hawaiians continued to create secular and sacred art after 1778 and 1819, and that objects collected by expeditions after Cook must be assessed in terms of possible influence from Cook's visit. These expeditions introduced new tools and ideas with the result that "evolved traditional art" includes "an upsurge of wooden image manufacture," especially in small images with props (stick images), images without props, and an occasional temple image. The stick images were often more finely made than those representing "traditional art" and may have been carved by individuals who did not have to depend on several persons to obtain and process materials such as for feather gods and large temple images (Kaeppler 1979:186). "Folk art" presumably is meant to cover what was produced after the era of large foreign expeditions had ended, but in their time both "traditional art" and "evolved traditional art" were part of "the living art of the community." "Tourist art" coexisted with "evolved traditional art" and "folk art" by 1825 when HMS *Blonde* visited the islands. Robert Dampier, artist on the ship, wrote (1971:47) of "plenty of trafficking" with the Hawaiians "bringing Idols, Shells, Stone axes, and other Curiosities, for which they invariably demanded a dollar." He adds, "Observing that several of us were

Introduction

eager to possess one of these ancient Idols they dilligently set to work, and soon fabricated a great number of grim looking deities. To these they endeavoured to give as ancient a look as possible hoping thus cunningly to impose on our credulity." A few years later Ruschenberger (1838:455) heard that when the demand for curios by the *Blonde* outstripped the supply, Hawaiians made objects and smoked them to look like antiques.

PART 1
DESCRIPTION OF MUSEUM PUPPET FIGURES AND HEADS

A. PUPPET FIGURES

1. Introduction

None of the ten manipulable wooden figures in museums has legs—only head, torso, and arms. Museums also have three separate wooden heads, perhaps once parts of assembled puppets; a fourth head known from a description is now missing. Two legless figures (only one with arms) and a torso are aberrant objects thought by some scholars to be parts of puppets.

All of these images are humanoid. No theriomorphic manipulable images have been reported except among present-day Hawaiian puppeteers. Winona Beamer, for instance, has a coconut-head puppet with tusks to represent Kamapua'a, Pig Child, who was a pig god and mischievous shape-shifter. Another puppeteer is said to have a manipulable image of a bird. Earlier Hawaiians may have had theriomorphic wooden puppets as indicated in two fictional narratives, to be discussed more fully in Part III. A little boy named Kaipalaoa, Sea Whale, won a contest with his hollow *pua'akukui,* a pig carved from kukui wood *(Aleurites moluccana),* and then further defeated his competitors with a magically dancing humanoid *ki'i* (Fornander 1917,IV:580ff.). A romantic saga tells how Chief Halemano, who was in love with a tabooed chiefess, got her little brother to arrange a meeting after bribing him with wondrous toys that included surf-riding wooden chickens *(moa)* and red-and-black humanoid *ki'i* (Fornander 1919, V:234ff.).

Theriomorphic wooden images also served religious purposes. Wooden images of a pig, or of its head only, were offered to Lono in a purification ceremony called *pua'akukui* after the image. Each landholding unit *(ahupua'a)* placed such an image on an altar *(ahu)* to be blessed by a priest and his companion who was a man-god. Chanting to Lono, the priest declared that the image would remain on the altar "until the vegetables rot in the fields" (because there would be too many to gather). These life-giving rites counteracted the life-destroying rites performed after completing a new *luakini*, the type of heiau where human sacrifices were made. (Malo 1951:163,179; Fornander 1919,VI:10.)

The figure of a plover *(kōlea)* was perched on the helmet of the massive wooden image that stood in front of a house inside the walled, tabooed precincts of 'Ahu'ena Heiau on Hawai'i (Choris 1822:Plate V). It is not known whether the entire image was carved in one piece or whether the plover and the head were separately made and attached with wooden pegs. The image represented Kōleamoku, Island Plover, sometimes regarded as an aspect of the great god Kāne. Kōleamoku was a deified chief and medical kahuna who specialized in treating acute illnesses. John Papa I'i's uncle, Papa, one of Kamehameha the Great's medical kahunas, included Kōleamoku and Lono (to whom 'Ahu'ena was dedicated) among his many benevolent and healing gods. (I'i 1959:45,123;Beckwith 1940:119;Malo 1951:109,111,note 11; Kalakaua 1888:50.)

These references to theriomorphic wooden figures, secular or sacred, emphasize that Hawaiian wood-carvers did not limit themselves to anthropomorphic forms, and that they may well have made manipulable puppets representing other than human beings. At present, however, museums have only the humanoid wooden puppets, now to be analyzed in detail as to their construction.

Museums have two structural types of puppets. One, represented only by a British Museum image, has a movable head separable from a hollow torso into which the neck is inserted, and separately made movable arms, each attached by a string, its free end hanging inside the torso and knotted with the other. The puppeteer reaches inside the torso to move head and arms. Each of the separate heads (two in England, one in Germany) was probably once assembled as a puppet with a torso and arms, and thus represented the same structural type as the British Museum assembled figure. The second structural type, represented by nine images in American museums, has a solid head and torso carved from one block of wood, with separately made arms, the only movable parts, fastened to shoulder projections by hinges of

Museum Puppet Figures and Heads

foreign materials. A puppeteer manipulates this structural type from outside the torso.

Dating is problematical for every example. Information is usually lacking on when it was made and collected, and even when a museum received it. The specimens in German and American museums being more obviously nineteenth century in origin are somewhat better documented than the very old-looking puppet heads in the British Museum.

2. British Museum Puppet

Labelled "idol" from the Sandwich Islands, the British Museum hand puppet (+249) has an unknown history except that the Reverend J. G. Wood (1880,II:442–443), after describing and sketching it, adds that he obtained it (year unreported) from "E. Randell, Esq.," probably a curio dealer who, Wood remarks, had supplied him with other artifacts. Wood may have had it well before the 1860s when the first volume of his book on the ethnography of primitive peoples of the world was published. In 1877 the Museum acquired it through Sir August W. Franks who had bought part of Wood's collection.

The assembled figure, approximately 52.07 cm. high, has four separate parts—two arms, a torso, and a long-necked helmeted head. Torso and head are each separately carved from unidentified light-weight white wood (wiliwili, *Erythrina sandwicensis?*). The entire figure, except for dogtooth fingers, is painstakingly and completely covered with a "skin" of tapa that has a grooved-beater pattern. The tapa, stained black with a brownish tinge, is pasted directly onto the wood. A strip of nearly white tapa of "much stronger and coarser texture" similarly covers the top of the helmet's median crest. According to Wood (p. 442), "The skill with which the maker has applied the cloth to the wood is really admirable. He has evidently soaked it until it was quite soft and tender, and by means of careful stretching and pressing has 'coaxed' it over the various irregularities—such as the nose, eyes, and mouth—so that it fits as closely as if it were the real skin." An

HULA KI'I: Hawaiian Puppetry

adhesive (breadfruit gum?) may have been used, as an exudation occurs around the arms.

With one exception, this is the only Hawaiian wooden image known to have tapa pasted directly on the wood. The exception, to be described later, is the British Museum separate head (Haw. 77) almost certainly collected in 1778 or 1779. Paste also secures the puppet's shell eyes in the eye sockets. Pasting was more often used than is generally recognized. For instance, the top layer of tapa on a fan in the Leningrad Museum Cook collection "is smeared with a pinkish white substance (glue?) which has retained here and there pieces of skin with red and yellow feathers . . ." (Rozina 1978:11,Fig. 23;12).

The puppet represents a paramount chief or king, for only he had the right to wear a crested helmet. However, the living chief (ali'i) had a twined helmet covered with red, yellow, and sometimes black feathers to wear with a feather cape or cloak. The style of the puppet's helmet, which has an elevated crescent crest and six spaced props, was less common than the wide-crested and the low-crested styles (Buck 1957:231–250). The puppet's crest narrows to a V above the forehead, widens across the top, narrows slightly at the back, and ends in a squared base on the neck. Each spoke differs in width and length. The three front spokes, thicker and longer than the other three, narrow unevenly down from crest to head. The rear three have more nearly equal measurements and are widely separated from the front spokes—perhaps a seventh spoke is missing. Crest, spokes ("rays"), head, and neck are carved, Wood (1880,II:442) thinks, from one piece of wood, but only an Xray can confirm this. The crest and perhaps the props may be separate pieces, judging from a damaged image (not a puppet) that retains vertical wooden pegs on top of its head that had once fitted into holes drilled in the base of its now missing crest (Buck 1957:476,Fig. 299b).

The British Museum, according to its record on the puppet, removed a rectangular, unpatterned, white tapa with brownish staining as "not belonging" to the figure, although Wood's sketch depicts it wrapped as a long skirt around the base of the torso. One wonders now how it had been fastened in place. The tapa

Museum Puppet Figures and Heads

"belonged," I believe, because it hid the puppeteer's upper arms when he inserted one hand into the hollow torso to move the head and arm-strings and raised the figure with the other. Moreover, an occasional Hawaiian image in museums still retains the tapa draped on it as a mantle, a malo, or a wrapping for storage.

The puppet's narrow head, oversized in relation to its torso, has a boldly modelled, hollow-cheeked, juttingly square-jawed, and very heavy-browed face with a prominent nose and large eye sockets containing narrow, elliptical mother-of-pearl shells secured with gum but with nothing applied to simulate pupils. Of the different techniques to inlay shell eyes, this technique, also present in the six National Museum puppets, is ignored in descriptions although it is used on numerous images. For instance, Buck (1957:472;473,Fig. 287c), who usually mentions when a roundheaded wooden peg secured a perforated shell eye and the round head became the pupil, comments on the pasting technique for only one example without considering its possible use on other figures. Further study may confirm that both the pasting and the pegging techniques for shell eyes existed in 1778 and that pasting is not necessarily a post-European innovation.

The puppet's ears are not shown. The open mouth in the prognathous lower face has tapa turned within it to imitate gums. It was added, Wood notes, after the teeth were inserted. The upper jaw has human teeth, the lower has sixteen palatine teeth from a large fish (shark?). A human tooth is visible at each corner of the mouth. I failed to ascertain how the teeth were attached, but usually carvers fitted each tooth into a small pit drilled inside the mouth (Buck 1957:470). Although many images have fish, human, dog, or wooden teeth, only this image has tapa-simulated gums.

The puppet's long, narrow, rounded neck tapers into a terminal peg that fits easily into a socket bored into the middle of the top of the torso. Still movable and removable, the solid head slides up, down, and around but not sideways unless one tilts the torso. Wood (1880,II:443) exclaims that "the variety of expressions gained by so simple an arrangement [altering the position of the head] is scarcely credible," and "whatever artistic power the

HULA KI'I: Hawaiian Puppetry

maker possessed has been given to the head, and it must be acknowledged that he has carried out his idea most vigorously."

A different head, if it fits into the socket, can be inserted, but the puppet is complete as it is. No other head will look "right" unless it is of the same scale and pasted over with the same color tapa. A staff member and I found that the separate head (Haw. 77) had too large a neck terminal to fit this socket. The other head (Haw. 76) was affixed to a display stand and could not be tried.

Like the nine puppets in American museums, this one shows no sign that the sculptor tried to make a realistically human torso. Instead he concentrated, like many other Hawaiian carvers, on the head and face. The shoulders and upper chest form a wide, flat, rounded area, which dips down and widens in front somewhat like an inverted triangle. Breasts are not indicated. The broad shoulders slightly obscure the holes for the attachment of the arms below them. The torso narrows slightly as if to form a waist, then widens a little and forms a rounded bole that can stand unsupported.

Each flexible, jointless arm is a tube covered with blackened tapa like the rest of the figure. The ragged right arm and left hand now expose the structure. "Rushes" (as Wood calls them) form the arms under the tapa. The material consists of vertical flexible strips of woody material (dried pandanus leaf?) overlaid with wider vertical strips. Each exaggeratedly large, stiff, triangularly-splayed, jointless hand—its cupped palm turned inward like many traditional images—is also of tapa-covered woody material. Each hand has six long, claw-like, dogtooth fingers. The shining white canine teeth are, as Wood writes, "a curious contrast with the black head and body." The huge hands and long, glistening, white nails are highly dramatic and visible when the arms are manipulated. The filling in the tubing tends to give the arms a curved look.

The question is: Why six fingers? Wood's conjecture that they symbolize extraordinary power has support from a daguerreotype of an unidentified kahuna with six fingers on his left hand (Archives of Hawaii; Scott 1968:194). This picture probably dates from the 1850s when J. J. Williams was a Honolulu photogra-

Museum Puppet Figures and Heads

pher. The kahuna may have belonged to the same six-fingered family that caught the attention of von Kotzebue (1821,III:151) on O'ahu during his first expedition. The puppet is unusual among Hawaiian images of any era in having dogtooth fingers; I know of no other examples.

A cord of vegetal material (perhaps olona, *Touchardia latifolia*, or hau, *Hibiscus tiliaceus*) passes from a hole in each arm through a matching hole under the shoulder; the two long free ends hanging inside the torso are knotted into a convenient loop for manipulation. Wood, strange to say, remarks on neither the hollow torso, the cords, nor the arm attachments. Obviously he never lifted the tapa drapery to discover that the torso is hollow and contains strings to control the arms. Now shoulders and arms have stuck together from gum seeping out from under the tapa pasted on them. To avoid damaging the arms and now fragile cords, a Museum staff member and I did not try to loosen them but experimented with the head. The image shows no sign of any structural or superficial alteration or repair since it was made. Despite the ragged arm and hand it appears to have been little used or used very carefully.

Its structure makes it obvious that the image functioned as an articulated hand puppet but whether for secular or sacred purposes can only be conjectured. It is classifiable as "evolved traditional art" rather than "traditional art" because of the virtual lack of documentation of its history. However, like "traditional art," its carver used only local materials and apparently only local tools and techniques, including the pasting of tapa on the wood and the assembling of the image from separately made parts. The two techniques may be stylistic variations present during the early historic period of which only this puppet and the datable separate head (Haw. 77) have escaped destruction. Other traditional elements are the pasting of pearl shell into eye sockets; the inserting of teeth into the mouth; the carving of a crested helmet (perhaps in parts and pegged into the head); and the loose tapa drapery.

My subjective impression is that a highly trained carver, following tradition, has conceptualized and carved a personalized creation that may reflect not only the stimulation of new ideas that came between 1778 and Kamehameha the Great's death in 1819, but the abandonment of the Hawaiian religion. By simplifying the form to essentials, the carver seems to express the essence of paramount chieftainship, of a ruler descended from the gods. The towering helmet-crest, the huge hands with claws, the mouth opened as if to orate or command, and the spare, almost skeleton-like face express dynamic alertness and authority.

What of other theories about the British Museum puppet? Cox and Davenport (1974:28,Fig. 3;29,135), who include it in the wooden sculpture produced within the fifty-year span after 1778, classify it as a "temple image," a term to designate one of "three classes of images clearly related to religious practices" (p. 50). In this class are the central and most important images in the tabooed area of a heiau as well as the auxiliary images either there or outside this area (p. 59). The image of the crested chief, they state (p. 28), "is similar in construction to the articulated marionettes that were part of certain hula performances . . . The two images with upraised arms in Choris's drawing of the Ahuena *heiau* . . . are apparently of this type." As I noted previously, the construction of the image differs somewhat from that of the National Museum puppets used in the hula.

W. T. Brigham (1898,Fig. 49;1913:290,Fig. 219) calls the image a "curious wooden idol with helmet . . . perhaps carried on a pole as was the god Kukailimoku; it was covered neatly with tapa like some idols from the Marquesas." Temple images were sometimes carried in processions outside the heiaus as, for instance, during the months-long Makahiki celebration when on one night the feather gods were paraded and on the next the wooden gods (Malo 1951:143). Carrying the puppet on a pole on any occasion seems unlikely, however, because of the mechanics of securing the pole inside the hollow torso and tying the head and arms to stabilize them. This after all would prevent their manipulation. Kūkā'ilimoku, mentioned by Brigham, was Kamehameha's personal god (aumakua) and war god. Kū, Snatcher of Islands, was often represented as a feather-covered wickerwork image and therefore was perhaps more conveniently transported on a pole (cf. Cox and Davenport 1974:88,Fig. 42;89).

Museum Puppet Figures and Heads

E. Dodd (1967:248–249), who puts this "helmeted warrior" among "Eccentricities" in his *Polynesian Art*, reports that at one time British Museum personnel called the puppet Pele for the volcano goddess because of a fancied resemblance to a wooden humanoid image in Paris in Musée de l'Homme (79-10-11) labelled "Iles Hawaii—la déesse Pele." No evidence supports the suggestion. The Paris image and a companion piece (No. 102 in Temple Square Museum, Salt Lake City) is quite different. It is a stick image (also called "image with a pointed prop") of a full figure carved with a pointed prop extending below its feet. The so-called Pele lacks a helmet; and the comb-like crescent crest, instead of resting on the head, rises from the base of the shoulders as "an arched overhead cover curving forward and downward over the face" (Buck 1957:484,Fig. 304e;485). Further, the Paris image is a full figure with flexed legs, and with its forearms resting on its thighs, something atypical in Hawaiian images.

Passing references with an illustration of the puppet are in the British Museum Ethnographical Handbook (1925:41,Fig. 39;166) which calls it an idol. Edge-Partington and Heape (1890,I:58,Fig. 2) have no comment about their sketch, and R. Poignant (1967: 52,53) describes the puppet as "a formidable image . . . probably meant to inspire fear."

Finally, here is the opinion of an artist, Jean Charlot, who moved to Honolulu where he studied Hawaiian culture and language, and produced paintings, murals, dramas, and other forms of art inspired by the islands. Writing in 1967 about Hawaiian sculpture in the British Museum, most of it gathered by explorers in the eighteenth century, Charlot states:

> I reproduce the head of an ancient marionette, used in the hula ki'i. The body is shaped so as to be held in the hand of the animator. The limbs are non-descript, being once hid under a chiefly cloak. There is something undoubtedly majestic in the stylized features topped by the heroically scaled helmet. This all-Hawaiian version of a warrior doubtless comes closer to the idea that Kamehameha the Great had of himself than does the pudgy bronze patterned after neo-clas-

HULA KI'I: Hawaiian Puppetry

sical statues that our legislators—when and if it is recast—are intent on inflicting on Washington.

Professor Charlot's reference to the hand puppet's limbs is doubtless due to an oversight, for the photo of the head he has reproduced is the familiar one from the Museum negative of the whole puppet without the draperies which once concealed the absence of legs. But the aesthetic effect of the dogtooth fingers on the arms would seem worth a comment. That the animator ever draped a chief's cloak over the figure is, of course, undocumented.

3. Nine Puppets in American Museums

(a) *Introduction.* Three puppets in the Bishop Museum and six in the National Museum of Natural History, Smithsonian Institution, are clearly nineteenth-century products, with the latter probably older than the former. Each has a personal name indicating its role, and is physically individualized as to face and head.

They are, however, basically similar in structure. Except for its arms, each has a solid head and torso cut from a single piece of soft, light-colored, light-weight wood, either wiliwili or kukui. The only movable parts are the separately made jointless arms nailed to broadly projecting shoulders by hinges of leather or cloth. Neither the flat-chested torso, minimally and roughly carved, nor the slightly better carved, more realistic but oversized head is hollow. The back of the head is flat, an admired trait emphasized on the living by molding an infant's skull. The face is broad, the toothless mouth a slit, and the sometimes flattened nose prominent, and the good-sized ears modelled. Pasted into the large oval eye sockets are either elliptical pearl shells or bluish-green earth to simulate mother-of-pearl—not, as one might first think, to imitate a Caucasian's blue eyes. Black foreign paint, occasionally covered with imported black felt or broadcloth, imitates hair, eyebrows, and sometimes the lower lids, and emphasizes ear helices and lobes. Traditional images also accent such facial features but in different ways. For instance, a feather-god image in Berlin Mu-

Museum Puppet Figures and Heads

seum für Völkerkunde (VI 253) has inlays of bunches of black feathers for eyebrows that meet and rims of the ears marked by yellow feathers (Eichhorn 1929:3).

Sexual differences are shown either by relative size or by some of the males having moustaches, sideburns, chin whiskers, or masculine hairstyles, all indicated with black paint or cloth or both. Two have head crests like helmets. Earlier in their careers, all puppets wore colored tapa garments. Now every puppet, male or female, wears a long gown fashioned from discarded foreign clothing that covers the torso and hides the puppeteer's hands. After European contact, men, proud to possess any item of imported clothing, sometimes wore ladies' gowns, a practice continuing into later times. An informant recalled in 1979 that her great-grandfather changed into a loose gown on coming home from his government position. In 1809, eleven years before the missionaries came, Hawaiian women in Honolulu wore whatever imported clothes they owned when they did the hula on festive occasions; the reason was not modesty but a desire to display all their finery (Campbell 1822:146–147).

(b) *Six National Museum Puppets*. Data about the history of the six National Museum images (USNM 258049–258054)—four males and two females—are from the Museum accession records and N. B. Emerson (1909:91–102), the major source on all hula, and from brief secondary accounts of *hula ki'i* by McPharlin (1969:15–17) and Malkin (1977:154,156,157–160;1980:18–19). On December 21, 1909, the U.S. Government Board of the Alaska-Yukon-Pacific Exposition, which had just closed in Seattle, transferred to the Museum (Accession 50958) 431 Hawaiian and other "South Sea" artifacts, including the puppets, purchased from Emerson. As nothing about these puppets appears in Seattle records on dramas in city theaters during the Exposition, they presumably were inactive and for display only.

The transfer records, which include part of the printed Exposition catalog and the original typed manuscript prepared perhaps by Emerson, add nothing that Emerson does not tell more fully in his book. It was published that same year by the U.S. Bureau of American Ethnology, the Bureau's first on a non-American Indian subject. An Act of 1906 had enabled it to broaden its scope and recognize that in 1898 the Hawaiian Islands had become a U.S. Territory, five years after Queen Lili'uokalani had been deposed. The accession records name only four of the six puppets, but data in Emerson's book enabled me to identify the unnamed female (258052) with certainty as Mailepākaha and the unnamed male (258054) as probably Kini Ki'i.

Emerson (1909:91) states in his very generalized account that he obtained the puppets (Nos. 314–319 in his personal catalog) "from a distinguished kumu-hula [hula master] who received them by inheritance, as it were, from his brother. 'He gave them to me,' said he, 'with these words, Take care of these things, and when the time comes, after my death, that the king wants you to perform before him, be ready to fulfill his desires.' "

He adds that "in the reign of Kamehameha III [1825–1854] they came into the hands of the elder brother, who was then and continued to be the royal hula-master until his death. These ki'i have therefore figured in performances that have been graced by the presence of King Kauikeaouli (Kamehameha III) and his queen, Kalama, and by his successors since then down to the time of Kalakaua. At the so-called 'jubilee,' the anniversary of Kalakaua's fiftieth birthday [November 19, 1886], these marionettes were very much in evidence."

Emerson, who gives neither the brothers' names nor the dates of their conversation, probably purchased the puppets after the fall of the monarchy.

I have not discovered when and where Kauikeaoūli's hula master got them, his name or that of his brother. Nothing points toward the puppets being the ones owned by Kaumuali'i's unknown hula master. In 1822, when Kaumuali'i moved to Honolulu after Liholiho (Kamehameha II) had stripped him of his relatively independent status as king of Kaua'i, Kauikeaoūli was only about eight years old and did not succeed Liholiho until the latter's death in 1824. As Kamehameha III reigned for thirty years, the period during which his hula master might have got the six National Museum puppets is very long.

The puppets may have performed for at least five Hawaiian

Museum Puppet Figures and Heads

monarchs—three Kamehamehas (III, IV, V), Lunalilo, and Kalākaua. We don't know whether Queen Lili'uokalani, in her brief and troubled stay on the throne, had the puppets perform for her, but, of course, she would have seen them at her brother's jubilee. Besides the six puppets, Emerson names three others of which he had heard, but it is not clear that they belonged to the same hula master. What became of them is unknown.

Each puppet, its head and body of one piece, has a disproportionately large head to make it more visible. None can stand unsupported because each has an uneven base. Each has pearl-shell eyes pasted into shallow sockets, and a roughly rectangular rather than rounded torso with wide shoulders. The haphazard, asymmetrical, and crude craftsmanship of head, torso, and arm stubs make my ten measurements on each image a mere approximation. Each side of a figure differs somewhat from the other. The height of the six ranges from about 30 to 35 cm., and the torso length (measured from the nape of the neck down) ranges from 13.5 to 18 cm. Torso circumference under the arms ranges between 15 and 22 cm., and at the base between 9.5 and 17 cm. Each arm stub differs, with length ranging from 2.5 to 5.5 cm. and circumference from 9.5 to 17.5 cm. Sometimes a slight cut on the shoulders (as on 258049) marks the articulation between the shoulder and the upper arm and the place where the hinge was to be fastened with metal nails.

The same or another carver made two of the male puppets (258053, 258054) later, I think, than the other four (two males, two females) who form a subgroup. The variant males show their difference in age in being of softer, yellower, differently grained wood and in having larger heads and faces. The grayish-brown paint on their faces may be less faded than the gray paint on the subgroup. One male (258053) has a head circumference of 41.5 cm., the other (258054), 40.5 cm.; the circumference for the subgroup ranges from 27 to 28.7 cm. Facial width from ear to ear is 16.5 cm. (258054) and 20.5 cm. (258053); for the subgroup the range is from 12 to 14 cm.

The two have variations of a *mahiole* (helmet) hairstyle imitated by an uncolored rectangle (258054) or an oval (258053) on the otherwise black-painted skull. Live men either bleached their hair with lime or shaved it to get the effect. By contrast, each puppet in the subgroup has a two-piece, black, cap-like foreign cloth stitched together and tacked down over the entire skull to imitate hair; and each male has a wooden crest like a helmet with the cloth cap fitted around its base. "The median line from the forehead over the vertex to the back-head is crested with the *mahiole* ridge," according to Emerson (1909:91). One male (258051) had his projecting medial crest (8 cm. long, 1 cm. high) carved down from the original block of wood to the top of his head. The other (258049) had his head gouged out and a semi-circular crest (12.5 cm. long, 1 cm. high), nailed into the cavity and wedged with pandanus leaf. It has now split. The different technique resulted either from a technical error or mishap, or he originally had no crest and it was later decided to make him a helmeted chief like the other puppet. This puppet's eyes, unlike the others, have black-painted pupils. Whether this was done to set him off from the other chief or whether all originally had pupils is unknown. Perhaps the paint has faded on the others. Blackening of the pearl shell to simulate a pupil is not unique. A stick image representing Kealoewa, a rain goddess (Bishop Museum 4044), has such pupils (Buck 1957:484,Fig. 304f;485–486).

Members of the subgroup are named for legendary or mythical characters. The two variant males are named for personality or status. Nihiaumoe, Midnight Prowler (258053), plays the role of lecher and ladies' man. Emerson (1909:94) sees the character further indicated by the extremely flat-backed head. The other male (258054), because of his very large face, very short neck, and purple gown, looks grave, authoritative, and solid. Unnamed in the accession records, he is, possibly, Kini Ki'i, King Image (*Kini*, Hawaiianized "King"). His appearance rules out his being Ki'iki'i, Snatcher or Apprehender, "a strenuous little fellow" (Emerson, p. 94), who carries out a chief's orders. Emerson merely lists Kini Ki'i by name.

The two helmeted chiefs, scarcely distinguishable at first glance, are Puapuakea (or Pupuakea), White Cock's Tail Feather (258051), and Makakūikalani, Royal Imaginativeness or Royal

Museum Puppet Figures and Heads

Boaster (258049); both are namesakes of legendary chiefs. The two females, Mailelauli'i, Small-leafed Maile (258050), and Mailepākaha, Blunt-leafed Maile (258052), are namesakes of two of four beautiful mythical sisters named for varieties of a fragrant green-leafed vine *(Alyxia olivaeformis)*; a fifth sister is named for a different plant. The puppet sisters are readily identifiable, not only because of their differently colored dresses but because Small-leafed Maile has a sterner look than her slightly smiling sister and a black stain like a bruise under her right eye. Also, each pearl-shell eye has four uneven holes drilled by the carver in the middle, as if originally meant for four-holed buttons; and her ears have a hole in front, as if for earrings. The sculptor has completely failed to show the two sisters' famous beauty.

The six puppets' arms are long unjointed tubes of white cotton cloth (Nihiaumoe has blue denim) turned inside out to hide closely stitched handmade or machined seams that slightly recall foreign dolls' arms. The material looks fresh enough to raise the question as to whether or not it replaced older imported cloth or even tapa as the "skin" to keep in the filling. The stuffing is dried, flexible, plant substances—folded coconut petioles, braided fibers, pandanus-leaf strips, and, for Nihiaumoe and Kini Ki'i, a yellowish fuzz from the base of a tree fern *(Cybotium sp.)* that Hawaiians once used to stuff pillows and mattresses. Each arm has a similarly made rather stiff hand with four or five barely indicated stiff jointless fingers. The slackness of each arm tube at the top is due either to shrinkage of the filling or to the animator's way of grasping it below the hinge that lengthens the arm to make it more visible to spectators, and connect it with the shoulder. These hinges—vertical strips of denim, felt, corduroy, flannel, or leather—are nailed to the stubs and stitched with black or white imported thread to the upper parts of the tubes. Some hinges have reinforcing bases of circular bands of imported cloth or cordage around both the tubes and the stubs.

This structural type requires more voluminous covering than the other structural type because it has no tapa pasted on it and the arms are not on strings. Draperies are required well up around the shoulders to hide the hinges, the unpainted crude torso, and the animator's hands as he moves the arms from inside the garments.

Now clad in layered garments of foreign cloth and style, the puppets, since they represent nobility, undoubtedly once wore the style Emerson (p. 92) describes only for Makakūikalani, namely, "a loose robe" of thin tapa called *māhuna*. This tapa, taboo to all but very high-ranking persons and made under strict taboos, is irregularly perforated with small holes *(kīkoi)*, and when dyed copper-color with juice from kukui-root bark is called *pa'ikukui*. Emerson's sample of Makakū's tapa was not found in the Museum collection.

Of Makakū's present costume, Emerson merely says that he "is now robed in a holokú of yellow cotton, beneath which is an underskirt of striped silk in green and white." Apparently he did not examine the costume closely to note the number of pieces and styles it includes. As he uses the term holoku for the original tapa robe and the present cotton caftan, one wonders just what style he meant. Pukui and Elbert (1957:73) define "*holokū* [as] 1. A loose, seamed dress with a train and usually a yoke, patterned after the Mother Hubbards of the missionaries." They distinguish it from a "*mu'umu'u*, which formerly was not yoked, and has no train or seam." Nowadays the puppets' elegant silk gowns might be called holoku and the yellowish caftan a muumuu, as many variations of both styles are still worn by Hawaiians and non-Hawaiians. In the early nineteenth century Hawaiian women sometimes had tapa fashioned into foreign-style costumes or added numerous wrappings of tapa to their gowns of foreign cloth and style. The puppets in American museums may have gone through similar fashion changes during their careers.

During the puppet's final active years, similarities in their costumes show that the same dressmaker and repairer worked on them. Each figure wears two or three layers of gowns and shifts, the longest more than three times the length of the torso concealed. The top layer, the same for all, is a loose, yellow-brown cotton caftan, most likely to imitate *pa'ikukui* tapa, that easily conceals the puppeteer's hands and protects, to some extent, the

Museum Puppet Figures and Heads

longer, elegant gown underneath. Perhaps it was removed for plays about post-European life in port towns. The caftan is slit at the neck and loosely stitched together at the sides. The shirred ends of the extra width which fall over forearms and wrists are on some dresses finished with wide, pleated ruching of the same material. Pinked or hemmed excess cloth at the neck is gathered in a ruff high under the chin by smocking or drawstrings covered with narrow, colorful ribbons or braid tied in bows.

The second layer, similar for all except Kini Ki'i, is a very long gown of fine foreign cloth in a nineteenth-century fashion. At their most elaborate, the gowns are high-necked and long-sleeved, with a fitted bodice and a full skirt ending in a train. One skirt, for example, has a combination of four pleated and unpleated vertical insets to add fullness; its train is formed by a long triangular inset starting at the shoulders. The two legendary chiefs and Nihiaumoe have gowns made from the same discarded silk taffeta dress, apparently originally white-striped Copenhagen blue, now faded to pale green. The ornamental braid is still blue and parts of the gown retain traces of the original color. Mailelauli'i's unhemmed gown is a blue and white plaid, setting her off from her sister clad in white with a small red design with a bright pink panel in front and trimmed with blue braid. Kini Ki'i, as befits his presumed status, wears a loose, royal purple robe of two pieces of cloth stitched together with white thread; the extra width over the arms is banded in bright red. The use of purple to symbolize royalty is a Western notion; Hawaiian nobility favored red and yellow.

Each puppet, except Mailepākaha, has a third layer, a white cotton shift next to the wooden torso; Kini Ki'i's better-made undergarment has set-in sleeves.

To imitate fancy, patterned gloves, each puppet has narrow strips of unhemmed white organdy, muslin, or gauze crisscrossing the hands from wrist to fingers. Gold, blue, or red ribbon or braid or scalloped embroidery fastened around the wrists catches the spectator's attention as the arms move. It also keeps the sleeves from sliding back to reveal the tubing. That the sleeves on Maka-

HULA KI'I: Hawaiian Puppetry

kū's shift are stitched right into the tubing suggests that his arms and shift may have been replaced at some time or that he was made later.

No puppet now wears jewelry, but Mailelauli'i, judging from threads remaining on her head, may have had an ornament, wreath, or hat sewn on her cloth hair; a hole in her ear may have been pierced for an earring. She still has a fragment of a narrow gold-braid band nailed into her mid-forehead that doubtless once encircled her head to simulate a yellow feather lei.

Puapuakea's wooden helmet, recalling a foreign palace-guard's headgear, has a vertical circlet of gold braid and fragments of yellow wool. His gold headband may simulate a feather coronet like one on Kaumuali'i's brow as he lay in state after his death in 1824 (Bingham 1847:223). Perhaps Makakū once had such a headband too, as fragments of one now hang around his neck. His wooden helmet also has bits of faded yellow wool of which Emerson (1909:91–92) comments that both the crest of his "*mahiole* ridge" and "its points of junction with the forehead and backhead are decorated with fillets of wool dyed of a reddish color, in apparent imitation of the *mamo* or *o-ó*, the birds whose feathers were used in decorating helmets, cloaks, and other regalia." Both the *mamo (Drepanis pacirica)* and the *o-ó (Acrulocereus nobilis)* were black with a few much-valued yellow or orange-yellow feathers.

All the puppets are now very dilapidated. The taffeta gowns are ragged. Puapuakea's broken neck has been partially repaired by winding cloth around it and nailing carpet tacks into rectangular leather strips, one in front, one in back, to reunite head and torso. (The resultant tilting of the head seems to add expressiveness.) A crack in Mailepākaha's back and head has nearly separated her torso and head. Her sister's head has a gouge either from termites or a fall. The puppeteer-costumer seeking for an overall effect was well aware that spectators cannot see details like mended bodies, mismatched thread colors, uneven stitches, or differently inserted dress panels. He succeeded admirably in making the six puppets look very handsome and eye-catching as they rose from behind their screen to dance the hula or act in plays for royalty.

Museum Puppet Figures and Heads

One can only guess whether this structural type originated at the same time or after the first type because although it can be produced and would, I think, be operational with only local materials, all examples use both imported and local materials. The structure is simpler than that of the first type in that the head and torso are an inseparable unit. This, however, resulted in loss of head mobility. Putting the arms on hinges that were nailed to the shoulders is also simpler than an alternative method of putting a cord through each arm and passing it through a hole cut under each shoulder (as in the first type). But since the torso was solid, a tunnel would have to be bored between the shoulders to pass the cords through and have them emerge for the puppeteer to handle through a hole cut in midback. The shoulder holes and tunnel through a solid torso, but not a hole in the midback, occur in a damaged, modern, Hawaiian "doll" (as it is labelled) in the Bishop Museum. (It will be discussed later.) Another simpler construction detail on the second structural type was to give the mouth minimal treatment to eliminate the need to insert teeth.

The structural type represented by the National Museum puppets is tentatively classifiable as "folk art" (to use Kaeppler's category) because these existing examples inextricably combine imported and native elements. Traditional pearl shell is pasted into eye sockets but nontraditional foreign paint and cloth highlight the facial features. Arm-tubes of imported cloth are stuffed with indigenous plant fibers. Older tapa was replaced by foreign-style clothing. Thus, the puppets combine old and new materials and ideas. That the puppeteer served upper-class society is shown in the quality of old foreign gowns he could get to dress his puppets. He has not hesitated to use any convenient material, local or imported.

Emerson's conjectures on the history of *hula ki'i* in the islands based entirely on these six puppets and others of which he had heard will be discussed in connection with conjectures by others about the Bishop Museum puppet trio.

(c) *Three Bishop Museum Puppets.* On August 13, 1914, Mr. E. Pa'akaula of Moanalua Valley, O'ahu, sold three puppets to Bishop Museum (B.221–223). He had received them from Nahai-

HULA KI'I: Hawaiian Puppetry

naka (unidentified), who had made them of wiliwili and used them in performances. Pa'akaula gave the names and sex of the puppets. The Museum made two photographs. One shows Pa'akaula sitting with his puppets; the other shows the puppets, arms outstretched, rising from behind a wide, light-colored tapa screen, with no manipulator visible.

Further information comes from notebooks, often undated and disjointed, started in the 1890s by Mrs. Gertrude MacKinnon Damon about the history and Hawaiian culture of Moanalua, a royal domain until 1884 when Princess Bernice Pauahi Bishop willed it to Samuel M. Damon. Jottings about puppetry date perhaps from around 1912 when six Moanalua puppets did the hula for William Alanson Bryan, Bishop Museum Curator of Ornithology. If the date is correct, his visit occurred two years before Pa'akaula sold the three puppets to the Museum. Perhaps the visit influenced his decision.

Below are some of Damon's scattered jottings on *hula ki'i*. Contrary to them, Pa'akaula brought three, not two, puppets to the Museum and they were of wiliwili wood, not of kou *(Cordia subcordata)*.

Pa'akaula, who lived back of Lehuawailele, was an employee on the Damon Moanalua estate. Mrs. Damon states that he

> was a noted hula teacher. . . . The hula kii was one of the dances of the olden time. This hula kii first spread in Waianae where it first originated. Paakaula learned it and when he had it, it came to Moanalua. Paakaula was the man who taught it to the Moanalua people. His pupils were Poloa, Kiliona, Kamakea (son of Haumana), Kamawaa and Pukui. There were six marionettes. One person had two marionettes and so on, dressed in various colors, red, yellow, pink, and so on. They looked very attractive. The drummers faced the spectators and a white sheet was spread behind them. When all was ready, the marionettes greeted all by bowing at the word 'aloha.' The marionettes began their act. They moved as in the hula when the chants were uttered.

Museum Puppet Figures and Heads

Damon then quotes a chant, "The Hungry Child," in English translation. It is given in Part II.

Another jotting in the Damon notebooks states:

> Kukuhoi came from Waianae, sister lived with a man in Moanalua. Kukuhoi taught Pakaula (man) the art of the Kii. Pakaula was a kumu hula and taught both boys and girls. Two of the dolls he owned are now in the Bishop museum, made of wood and very heavy. Naked figures of a boy and girl, when used they were clothed in tapa and later on in more modern clothes.

Another note repeating some of the information above says of Pa'akaula's "two kii hulas" that

> they were made of wood possibly kou, very heavy—naked figures of a boy and girl—very sacred—scared to touch it. Pakaula was a well known hula teacher—he and Nohoanu (Namakahelu's sister and Kipi's first wife).

Other details are also repeated occasionally. It is not clear if Hui, another hula master, apparently older than Pa'akaula, was also a puppeteer.

It is also not clear when during the latter part of the nineteenth century puppetry was introduced, or perhaps reintroduced, into Moanalua Valley. It may have been practiced secretly for a long time only for Hawaiian audiences after hula came first under mission-inspired taboos and later under laws of the Legislature. That Wai'anae had puppetry before the 1880s is suggested by the discovery in 1881 of a detached wooden head, perhaps of a puppet, in a Wai'anae heiau and now in the Berlin Museum. What became of the six Moanalua puppets is unknown.

Pa'akaula's three puppets, obviously a family, consist of an adult male *(kāne)* named Makaalei (Mākālei), Magical Fish Stick; an adult female *(wahine)* Kawehiokanāhele, The Adornment of the Forest; and a male infant *(keiki kāne)* Hi'ilani, Nursling.

HULA KIʻI: Hawaiian Puppetry

The basic structure of the three is like that of the six National Museum puppets—head and torso carved as a unit and arms made separately and attached by hinges nailed to wide shoulders. The three, however, have a rounded torso that narrows sharply and progressively below the shoulders as a handle for the puppeteer to grasp with one hand while moving the arms with the other. No torso can stand alone because it is top-heavy and has an uneven base, perhaps to be thrust into the ground.

Measurements on the unevenly carved figures are approximate. Sex was reported by Paʻakaula and is shown only in differences in head size, total height, and shoulder width. Each has a large, flat-backed head; the adult male's is over twice the size of the female's. His total height is 51.5 cm.; 30 cm. of that is below the neck. The female appears smaller but her total height is about the same with slightly more of her length below the neck than is the case with the male. Unlike his rounded torso, hers is flat and thin. She is 15.5 cm. across the shoulders; he is 24.5 cm. The infant is about 37 cm. tall with 21 cm. of his height below the neck. In every way he is smaller than the adults. His torso is now much deteriorated around the base.

The female's arms, unlike the males', are slats, each 28.5 cm. long and approximately 4.5 cm. wide, cut from a produce box. The left still bears large black print with words like WELL VENTILATED; the right has THIS SIDE UP. KEEP COOL AND. The males' arms are of heavier lumber, also imported. No two arms have the same measurements. Mākālei's right, for example, is 23.5 cm., the left, 21.25 cm.; each is 4 cm. wide and 2 cm. thick. The infant's right is 24 cm. long, the left, 21 cm.; each is about 3 cm. wide and 2.5 cm. thick.

The female's slat arms have leather hinges; the males', green baize or felt, salvaged perhaps from a billiard table. When I first saw the puppets years ago at the Museum before they were dismantled for reasons of preservation, the males retained pieces of older leather under the baize, evidence of much use and repair. The variety of nails fastening arms to hinges and hinges to arms included carpet tacks (some with old-fashioned squared heads) and shingle and picture nails.

Museum Puppet Figures and Heads

The two adults have oval eye sockets. The adult male has no fillings now, lost perhaps before he reached the Museum, and the female's bluish-green earth (now faded to gray) was probably inserted with glue of some kind into the sockets. The infant has two empty small holes bored near his nose and has a beady look. Each mouth is toothless, deeply cut, small and pursed-looking. Each has a large nose with nostrils bored open except in the infant whose nose is flatter and less aquiline than the adults. Ears are large, raised, and crescent-shaped. Shiny black paint simulates short hair; the eyebrows are less dark than the hair, and the three puppets have splotches of black around the sides of the face. The faces are unpainted but that of the female looks gray. Mākālei, the adult male, has on his upper back some black marks vaguely resembling a footprint; the significance is unknown but perhaps it is the owner's personal mark.

Mākālei weighs 1085 grams, the female, 880 grams, the infant, 400 grams. The weight given is without their clothing which was very light anyway. When I first saw the images, each wore a roomy poncho of beige cotton with small brown polka dots recalling *māhuna* tapa. The garment was made by folding over the cloth, cutting a V-shaped slit in the middle for the neck, and letting the open sides fall, unfastened, over the wooden arms. The nonfunctional seams are clearly left from the cloth's former use. Common pins in the garments may have been added later to secure the necklines; a puppeteer would not risk pricking himself.

Obvious errors of fact about Pa'akaula's puppets which were confused with the six National Museum puppets, occur in a report attributed to Mary Kawena Pukui (Costa 1951:142):

> *Marionettes or Puppets.* The marionettes or puppets that are mentioned by Emerson are now in the Bishop Museum. They are probably not indeginous [sic] to Hawaii as Emerson reported, for none of the very old Hawaiian dancers and dancing masters had ever heard of them, before these were made. A man by the name of Paaluhi made these, and he probably fashioned them after the Punch and Judy shows. A woman who saw a performance of them said that one of the

HULA KI'I: Hawaiian Puppetry

things they were made to do was to put the arms before the face and move them as if they were wiping away tears. The dolls are made to look Hawaiian. The heads are made of a soft wood and the eyes of steel [shell?]. The body, under a pink muumuu, is made of what looks like apple crates. The printing is still there.

A later account also mistakenly identifies Emerson's puppets with Pa'akaula's (Barrère 1980:41,55). (Pa'akaula's puppets, to reiterate, are in the Bishop Museum, Emerson's in the National Museum.) Nahainaka, not "Paaluhi," carved the Bishop Museum puppets, and used crating only for the female's arms and no pearl shell for any of the eyes. Because some very old Hawaiian entertainers had not heard of Hawaiian puppets before Emerson's or Pa'akaula's (which is meant is unclear), probably Kaumuali'i's puppets had been forgotten.

The reference to a pink muumuu is supported by Mrs. Damon's comment that the Moanalua figures once wore colored garments but she does not describe the style or material. The remark that the puppets wiped away tears is interesting because the only chant Mrs. Damon mentions is about a crying orphan.

The statement that the puppets were fashioned after Punch and Judy shows is probably derived from Emerson's two references to them rather than from tantalizing resemblances. For instance, Punch and Judy had a squalling Baby (perhaps a nineteenth-century addition to the English cast, according to Speaight 1970:86) and thus constituted a family like the three Bishop Museum puppets. The male infant, Nursling, recalls Baby in name and crying. However, the chant calls for Nursling to be comforted whereas Punch threw the squalling Baby out the window.

Although I have found no record of a professional Punch and Judy show in the islands before 1970 when the McDonald's restaurant chain had a Punch and Judy booth as a promotional feature, it would have been familiar to both foreign and Hawaiian nineteenth-century residents through travel, reading, and hearsay. Mrs. Damon was probably familiar with it, for she was born and reared in Scotland. Punch was in London by 1662, in Philadelphia by 1742, and in San Francisco by the 1850s when many islanders joined the Gold Rush. In 1869, fifteen-year-old Walter E. Deaves (who in 1884 and 1912 brought an elaborate marionette troupe to the islands) had his own Punch and Judy booth on San Francisco streets (McPharlin 1969:268–273). Punch, Judy, and Baby may, I think, have contributed new elements to Moanalua puppetry but not until late in the nineteenth century.

Emerson (1909:91) refers so ambiguously to the possible influence of the Punch and Judy show on the ultimate origin of *hula ki'i* that it is uncertain whether he means the show with the famous couple or puppetry in general, for the term "Punch and Judy" is often used as a synonym for any kind of puppetry. For instance, on November 29, 1886, the *Pacific Commercial Advertiser* (Frowe 1937:130) called *hula ki'i* the "ancient Punch and Judy of the Hawaiians." Emerson wonders if *hula ki'i* is an "imitation of the Punch-and-Judy show familiar to Europe and America," but decides that there is no evidence "other than what might be inferred from a general resemblance, for the theory of adoption from a European or American origin. On the contrary, the words used as an accompaniment to the play agree with report and tradition, and bear convincing evidence in form and matter to a Hawaiian antiquity. That is not to say, however, that in the use of marionettes the Hawaiians did not hark back to their ancestral homes in the southern sea or to a remoter past in Asia."

The play he refers to may be the one he later discusses (and I describe it in Part II) in which the two Maile sisters and the two legendary chiefs act in a plot based on orally transmitted narratives. Of course the play could have been composed at any time in the post-European period and is not necessarily ancient because of its subject matter.

Emerson (p. 98) quotes one of his principal informants (Mrs. Jenny Wilson, 1872–1962), who included imitations of puppets dancing in her repertoire, as saying "that she witnessed for the first time the European counterpart of the hula ki'i, the 'Punch and Judy' show" in Berlin, near the end of her four-year tour late in the nineteenth century in America and Europe. Again it is not

HULA KI'I: Hawaiian Puppetry

clear whether she saw a real Punch and Judy show or some other puppets or marionettes. She was probably familiar with Hawaiian royal puppets, for she grew up in court circles, and at age fourteen or so she was chosen by King Kalākaua to join a troupe of young hula dancers to perform at his private parties. Her maiden name was Kini Kapahukula-o-Kamamalu Huhu. (Mellen 1952; Kealiinohomoku 1964.)

On July 22, 1978, the Bishop Museum sent Pa'akaula's puppets to Moanalua for a visit, but in display cases attended by two Museum escorts. They were inactive but some newly made puppets in human and animal form, structurally different from those in museums, acted in Hawaiian plays in a puppet booth or danced on the open stage on the hands of live performers under the direction of Winona Beamer, hula master and puppeteer. Their performances creatively combined native Hawaiian and foreign elements of puppetry.

The occasion was the Prince Lot Hula Festival to honor the memory of Prince Lot Kapuaiwa (1830–1872), one of the former owners of Moanalua. In his younger years, Lot had actively encouraged the revival of hula "in or near Moanalua. Hula practice sites sprang up from Moanalua to Ewa; Prince Lot gave frequent parties for members of ships' companies at his 'place in the country,' now known as the Kamehameha V Cottage in Moanalua Gardens. Hula performances were often a feature of these parties" (*Na Makani o Moanalua* 1978: March).

The Festival organizers conveniently overlooked that Lot later got the Legislature to pass a law requiring a license to teach or do the hula because Hawaiians on his lands and elsewhere neglected their means of livelihood for hula. As Minister of the Interior he granted no licenses for performances outside Honolulu (Lyman 1895:15–16;Kuykendall 1953:125,153).

Nonetheless, when he became King Kamehameha V (1863–1872), one of his many critics, the Reverend Oliver P. Emerson (1928:209), deplored his heathenism, the number of licensed kahunas, the upsurge of licentiousness, the reappearance of a gross type of hula, and corruption, which, Emerson concluded, was later surpassed only during Kalākaua's reign.

Museum Puppet Figures and Heads

The three Moanalua puppets, the only existing assembled puppets from rural O'ahu, were probably carved in the late nineteenth or early twentieth century, with the structural type suggested most likely by the royal puppets, in view of Moanalua's long association with royalty. The notion of having a family unit may reflect familiarity with Punch, Judy, and Baby. The three Bishop Museum puppets like the six in the National Museum, represent "folk art."

1. Old California playbill, circa 1850s. (Hawaii State Archives)

GREATEST ATTRACTION
OF THE SEASON
CHARLES DERBY .... Proprietor

KANAKA!
DANCING GIRLS

The Celebrated Sandwich Island

HULA! HULA!
LADIES PROHIBITED
FIRST TIME IN CALIFORNIA

The Wonderful Performers will make their First Appearance on

This Troupe of Hawaiians consists of the following:
WAHINES OR DANCING GIRLS:
Hoo-kie-kie and Keo-ho-hi-na.

KANAKA DRUMMERS AND CHANTERS:
Ka-na-au,
Kaa-mo-ku,
Na-o-ni-hi-ni-hi,
Ne-wa,
Ka-i-li.

PART I.
Pule ia Laka ke Akua!
Prayer to the Hawaiian Deity who presides over Dancing

HULA PAIPU!
Ke hookikii mai nei ke opua Lani
Chanting and Drumming

CHANT!
Look on us Oh! Cloud from Heaven!

HULA! OLAPA!
Dancing Girls enter and go through the

KUALOLOA!

PART II.
Puili or the Bamboo Dance
HULA KII
— OR THE —
DANCE OF THE PUPPITS

The Performance will conclude with the exciting and wonderful HULA HULA

HIIUALANI!!

Hele mai hookahi! hele mai a pau,
e nana i ka poe Hawaii.

Admission - - Fifty Cents.

2. *A Man of the Sandwich Islands, Dancing.* (Louis Choris, 1816)

3. *Ahu'ena Heiau, Hawaii.* (Choris)

4. *An Offering before Capt. Cook in The Sandwich Islands.* (John Webber, 1778)

5. "Idol." British Museum puppet with tapa skirt. (J. G. Wood sketch, 1877.)

6. Disassembled British Museum puppet. (Ben Burt photos)

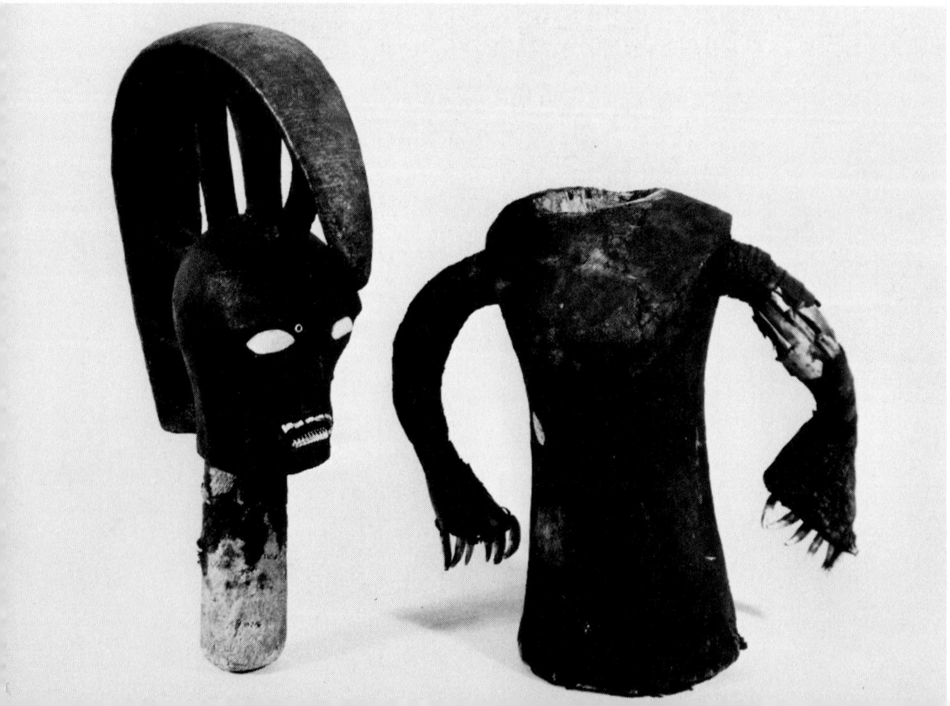

7. The assembled British Museum puppet.

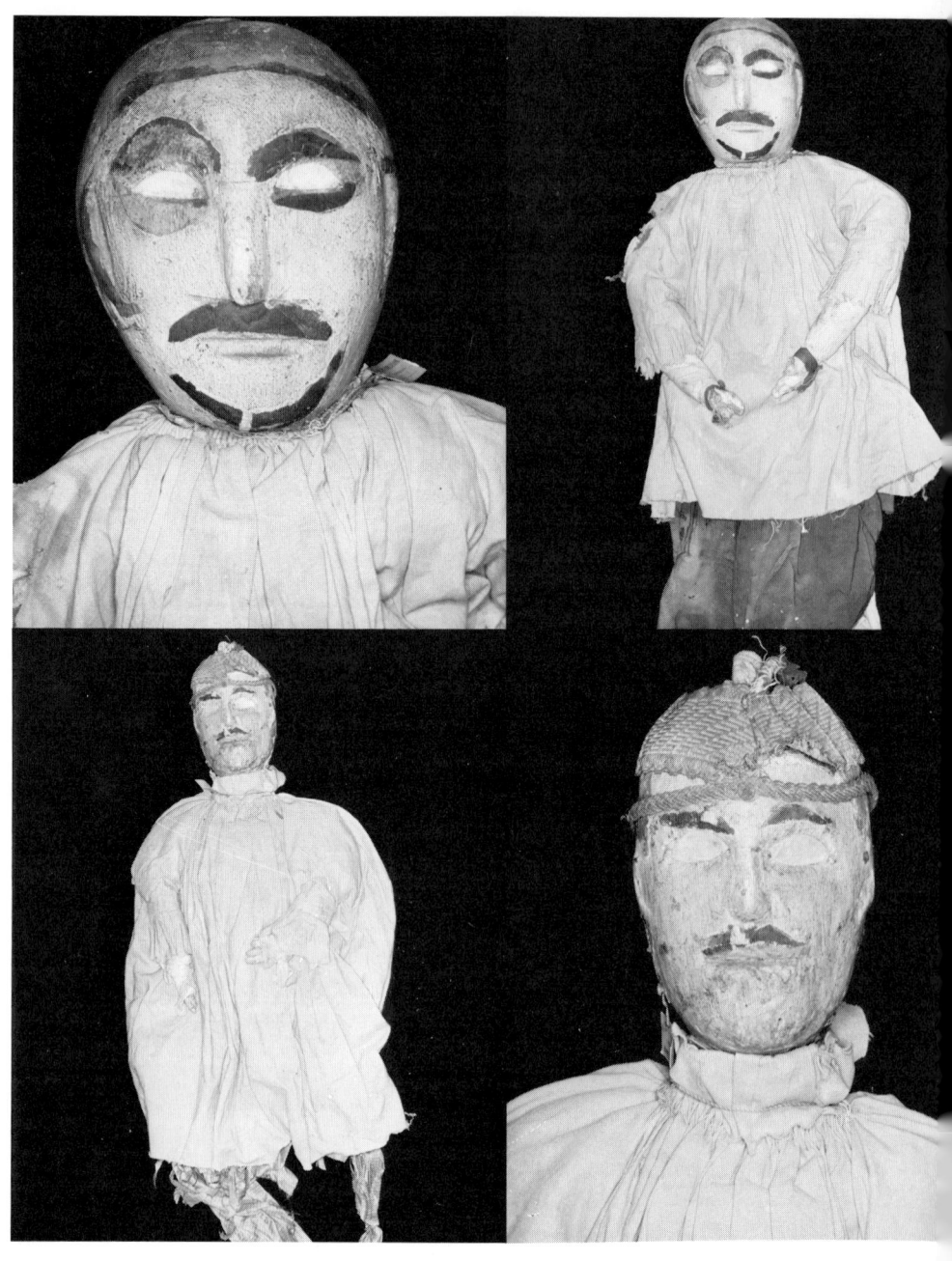

8–9. Kini Ki'i or "King Image." National Museum of Natural History, Smithsonian Institution. (Martha Cooper photos)

10–11. Puapuakea or "White Cock's Tail Feathers."

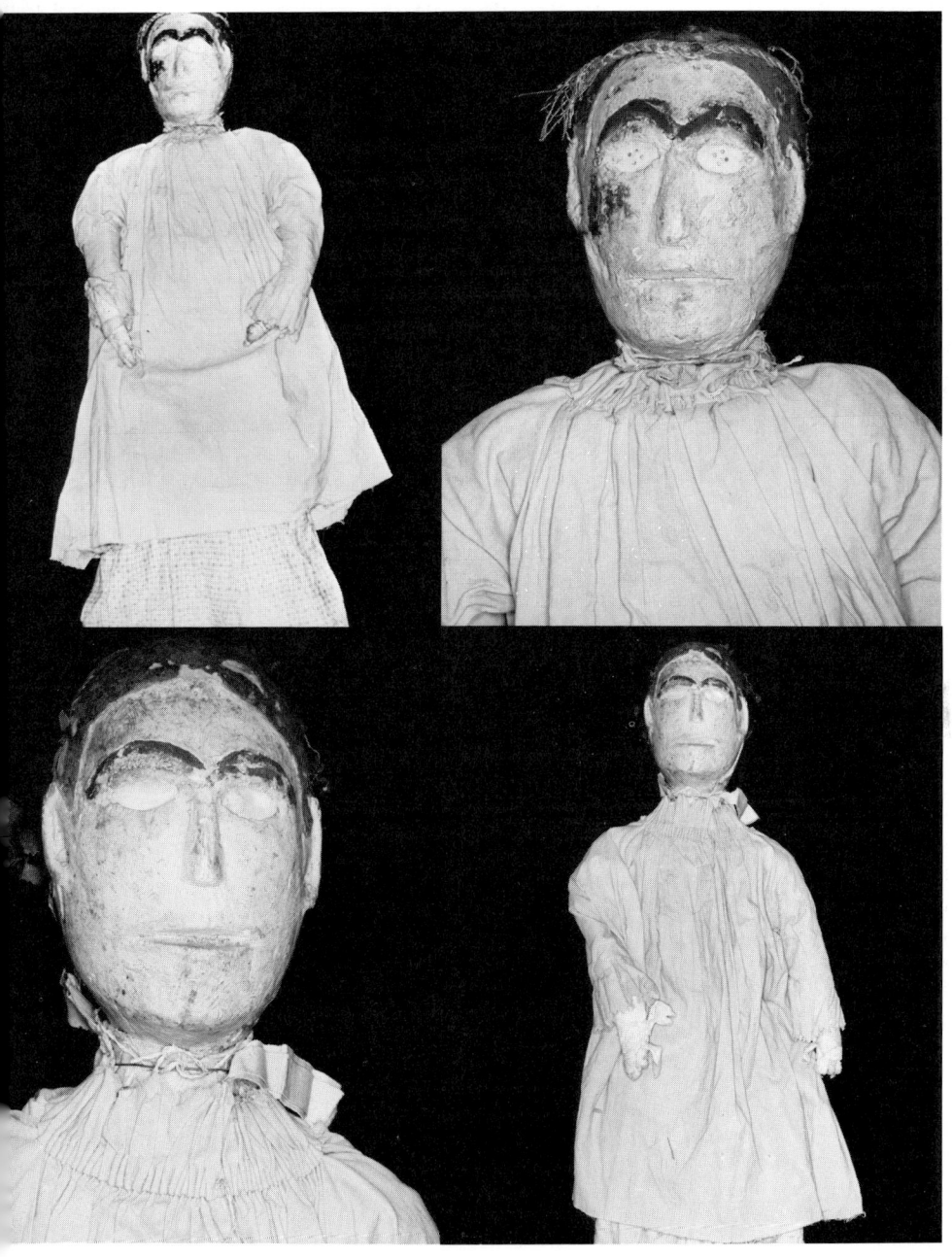

12–13. Mailelauli'i or "Small-leafed Maile."

14–15. Mailepākaha or "Blunt-leafed Maile."

16–17. Makakūikalani or "Royal Boaster."

18–19. Nihiaumoe or "Midnight Prowler."

B. TWO ABERRANT BISHOP MUSEUM IMAGES

1. Introduction

Bishop Museum has two poorly documented figures, legless humanoid images, that one staff member considers to be puppets but which seem to me unusable as such. Although accession records call one a "doll" and the other a "puppet," their function is unknown but they certainly represent carvers' experiments in "folk art."

2. The "Doll"

No information accompanied "Hawaiian doll of *hau* wood" (B.2821.H.1) received in 1921 from the S. M. Damon Estate and presumably made at Moanalua. This humanoid, uncovered, unpainted figure, approximately 15 cm. long and 8 grams in weight, consists of a head and torso cut as a unit from *Hibiscus tiliaceus* (hau). It has now lost one of its tiny, deformed-looking arms that once fitted into rectangular holes cut in the torso. The crude, paw-like hand of the existing arm (now detached) has tiny nicks to simulate fingers. Underneath the torso, cut down from the wood, is a toothpick-thin, spindle-like stick, perhaps intended to fit into a socket in a piece of wood, either the base of a whirligig or the nether extremities of a complete figure.

At the back of the head is an oval raised area (4 cm. long and 1 cm. wide), which extends to the neck and looks more like a chignon than a low crest. The oval and shallow eye sockets were probably never filled. The nose is long, flat, and wide. Inside the open mouth (accented by shaving the wood against the grain) the wood has been cut to imitate three teeth. A slight raised area on the right side of the head may be an ear; a rough place on the left may be the remains of one.

The short neck merges into sloping shoulders and a broad chest with two roughened spots as if raised nipples had broken off. The figure then narrows to a flat round base with the spindle.

HULA KI'I: Hawaiian Puppetry

Under the right shoulder a rectangular armhole (2 cm. long, 1 cm. wide) has a lightened area following the curve of the bust and the straight line of the back. The left armhole is rough and broken—the carver, it seems, had trouble with the soft wood on the left side of the figure. The broad end of the short, unrealistic, existing arm exactly covers the armhole and terminates in a plug inside the bust, which is hollow between the armholes. Through a tiny hole in the middle of the plug and each side of the armhole, the carver inserted a very thin stick as an axle but it was too fragile to work, as sharp, broken bits of wood left in the holes show. Two tiny holes on each side of the plug may have been strung with fine thread or wire through the tunnel to connect with the other arm. The arms would have had very limited movement. No opening exists in the back of the torso through which string could have emerged to move the arms more freely.

The "doll" is a fragile example of inventive "folk art" using native and foreign ideas of realism.

3. The "Puppet"

On February 26, 1973, Bishop Museum received from Miss Amy Greenwell of Hawai'i "One puppet. Carved wood figure, with necklace of white shells. Head has carved features, round body, no limbs, hourglass shape with flat bottom. Tag taped on reads 'Hula Ki'i, 53. A. G.' Address tape: Miss Amy Greenwell taped to bottom also. 27.5 cm. high, 7 cm. wide. Hawaiian Islands." (No. 1973.36.)

The uncovered, unpainted figure, of dark, close-grained, unidentified wood, weighs 390 grams. No evidence exists on the head and torso cut from one piece of wood that the figure ever had or was intended to have additional parts. The front and back of the torso are flat, the sides rounded. Shallow cuts simulate eyebrows above small, shallow eye sockets, not intended to be filled. A small black stain under the left eye is the only color added to the figure except for white marks in places around the head. The nose is aquiline while the closed mouth has upturned corners as if in a smile. A small round hole on the left side of the head was

Museum Puppet Figures and Heads

drilled either by the carver or an insect; long, deep cracks on the figure may be due to drying out of the wood.

The former owner left unexplained why she called this a *hula ki'i*. The only way it could be used in hula would be to hold it and chant to it. It may have been a symbol of someone's personal god or a decorative object. Regardless, it is classifiable as modern "folk art."

C. A TORSO AND SEPARATE PUPPET HEADS IN MUSEUMS

1. Introduction

Three separate, wooden heads of men, which, I think, were once parts of puppet figures like that in the British Museum, are in London and Berlin museums. A fourth, like them, collected by one of the Bloxam brothers in 1825, is missing but known from a published sketch and brief description. These heads differ from the well-known type of portable Hawaiian image made of feather-covered twined work that consists only of a grotesque humanoid head and neck, the latter wide enough at the base for the image to stand (Buck 1957:503–505). The type represented by the four wooden heads has a long neck, its end without cordage, paint, pasted tapa, or other ornamentation because it is invisible when inserted into the socket of a torso.

Why are there no existing torsos for such separate heads? If the torsos were crudely carved because covered with tapa drapery, they may have been more readily discarded by the manipulator or the collector than the better carved more realistic heads. The British Museum puppet probably retained its parts because the tapa pasted all over its head and separate arms and torso gave it a unified appearance.

2. Berlin Museum Torso

The only existing separate torso—if it is indeed a torso—is in the Berlin Museum für Völkerkunde (VI 8376) which it reached through Dr. Eduard Arning. Islanders had found it in 1880 near Laupāhoehoeiki, Hāmākua, Hawai'i, in a rock-lined, rock-covered cavity with a kneeling kou-wood image (VI 8375) and a human skull (Eichhorn 1929:5–8,Figs. 7,8;Arning 1931:68–69).

Cox and Davenport (1974:193l), remark that the torso may have been "used for the base of an assembled image, as in . . . [British Museum + 249], or possibly as the body of a marionette." They also note the existence of the two separate heads in the British Museum and that missing from the Bloxam collection. They think that the torso "was probably covered with tapa. . . ." However, its structure, as I shall show, is such that it could not have been part of an assembled image; it symbolizes a goddess who may have been depicted in the form of this object; and if it ever had tapa either loose or pasted on it no trace now remains.

The object referred to as a torso or bust *(Herme)* in the earliest description (Eichhorn 1929:7) is roughly carved in the round probably from breadfruit wood. The right shoulder, for instance, is higher than the left. The very wide-shouldered, flat-chested, and narrow torso, which widens toward its circular base, is 92 cm. long. It has a circumference of 55 cm. at its narrowest part. It has a V-shaped notch cut just off center at the top in front. Coconut-wood pegs form a pattern on the surface. Such an image was customarily kept in a wickerwork, house-shaped container decorated with feathers and greenery, and as traces on the torso show, its former caretaker *(kahu)* anointed it with coconut oil and ochre *('alaea)*.

The back has been so hollowed out that the torso is like a wooden shell; the long, narrow, reddened opening extends from the very top of the back to just above the base. The cavity probably served as a storage place for the worshipping caretaker's equipment. Images with similar openings are often called *kālaipāhoa* (carve-stone axe) after the notorious poison god Kālaipāhoa of Moloka'i whom Kamehameha the Great added to his pantheon. A sorcerer kept his death-dealing bait in the opening (Buck 1957:472;473,Fig. 297). However, other non-malevolent sacred images also had similar openings; the kneeling image found with the torso, for example, had a cavity in the back of its head (Buck 1957:477,478). Structurally the wooden torso could not have been part of an assembled image because the cavity is so wide and extensive that it could not have held a head securely; further, the object has no openings for arms.

The torso, Arning learned, represents Kāmeha'ikana. This name, meaning Wondrous, was given to the usually benevolent primal earth goddess Haumea (also called Papa) after she either transformed herself into a breadfruit tree or entered the trunk of

Museum Puppet Figures and Heads

one to hide herself and her companion from pursuers. These pursuers later used some of the wood to make an image of her as Kāmeha'ikana. She was then worshipped on O'ahu and later on Maui. She became one of Kamehameha's deities because she could win land, power, and stable government for him. (Beckwith 1940:276-290;I'i 1959:44.) As Haumea, the goddess continually renews her youth to bear innumerable children, assist women, and perform marvels with her magical branch or stick called Mākālei. (This name, it will be recalled, is also that of the Bishop Museum male puppet.) The wooden torso, with its large opening and vague resemblance to a human shape, may represent the goddess in the process of transforming herself into a breadfruit trunk. Or she had already transformed herself, or the live tree was opening up to receive her. Perhaps this female image and the one found with it had belonged to a high-ranking chiefess who had worshipped the goddesses they represent.

The female kneeling-image with Kāmeha'ikana symbolizes Kihawahine, another famous goddess, according to residents near the site. Kalākaua, however, identified her as Papa but could not explain her posture, which is atypical for images (Brigham 1898: 16,note). Local residents probably identified her correctly. Kihawahine, originally a Maui chiefess and ancestress of Ke'ōpūolani, Kamehameha the Great's sacred wife, was transfigured at death and worshipped as a powerful guardian god (aumakua) by her descendants. Kamehameha adopted her as one of his gods, and an image of her was carried in Makahiki processions. She sometimes took the form of a lizard or water spirit *(mo'o)* and with Haumea was among the major goddesses worshipped particularly by chiefesses (cf. Malo 1951:82,116;I'i 1959:44;Kamakau 1961:166,179,180). When the two images and the skull were brought from their burial place to Waimano, residents became afflicted with white flecks on their lips, mouths, and other parts, which a kahuna attributed to the sacrilege of taking these objects from their resting place.

It is likely that the torso of Kāmeha'ikana found on Hawai'i was never intended to be part of an assembled image, in view of the myths and beliefs about the goddess having entered or trans-

HULA KI'I: Hawaiian Puppetry

formed herself into a breadfruit tree. The torso could not have supported a head, and there are no armholes.

3. British Museum Head (Haw. 77)

The two separate wooden heads (Haw. 76, Haw. 77) in the British Museum look old. One (Haw. 77) was surely collected by Cook's third expedition because in 1783 Miss Sarah Stone made a watercolor sketch of it (Force and Force 1968:101), and the English did not revisit the Hawaiian Islands again until the expeditions in 1785–1788 of Nathaniel Portlock and George Dixon, who had been with Cook in Hawai'i. Sarah Stone was commissioned by Sir Ashton Lever to make watercolor sketches of some of his collection. At an unknown time the Leverian Museum, London, which housed Lever's collection after 1774, had acquired the head she depicted. After the Leverian collection was dispersed in 1806, the head reached the British Museum at an unknown time before 1880, as its type of number reveals. The origin other than the Sandwich Islands is unknown.

The head, about 29.2 cm. high, is, according to Museum records:

> . . . probably of an idol carved in very soft wood and represented as wearing a low crested helmet. The face is covered with brown kapa, but the nose is covered with a piece of some animal's skin to which some brown fur still adheres. The eyes are formed of pointed oval pieces of pearl shell perforated in the center: the left eye has a lump of kapa in the perforation. The open mouth is set irregularly with shark's teeth. The top of the helmet-crest is covered with twisted fibre-cord, the strands of which are alternately brown and black. The cap of the helmet is represented by a broad binding of the same cord passing across the temples and down the back of the head. A band consisting of five strings of the same cord, runs from the back of the head across the upper lip, and the neck is bound for some distance with the same,

Museum Puppet Figures and Heads

the lower part however being bare wood and apparently in two pieces, one of which is cylindrical and perforated vertically. The sides of the helmet-crest were originally covered with patches of the skin of some small animal (rat?) overlaid with dark brown kapa; but on the left side the kapa has entirely disappeared, while on the right side the lower three quarters are intact. Two ends of the black and brown cord hang loose from the base of the helmet.

The head has unusual features, rare or absent in other existing Hawaiian images. No other known image has been reported with animal skin and fur on it, least of all with an overlay of tapa. Pre-European sources were the now extinct native dog and rat. The rat was brown as were some dogs. However, no use of rat hide or fur has been reported, but dogskin with hair attached, especially long white hair, was used on the tip of wands for rituals and games (Buck 1957:366–367), and may have been added to men's hair ornaments. A second unusual feature is the extensive coverage of the head with black and brown cord. A third feature, familiar from the British Museum puppet, is the tapa pasted on the face and helmet crest. The tapa plug in the left eye may have replaced the broken head of a wooden peg that had simulated the pupil and secured the shell in the eye socket. The technique was to insert the pointed stalk of a roundheaded wooden peg through a single central perforation in the shell and force it into a pit made with a pumpdrill. The external round head of the peg imitated a pupil (Buck 1957:470;471,Fig.296d). On some images the pupils were painted; a feather image in Berlin Museum für Völkerkunde (VI 253) has wooden pupils colored blackish green (Eichhorn 1929:3). In some images which have a seed as a pupil, the seed may have been put into a perforated shell or pasted on outside, with the shell itself probably pasted into place. More information is needed on the subject. The eyes of Haw. 77 are much larger than the British Museum puppet's which are glued into place rather than pegged. An unusual feature on Haw. 77 is the two-part neck of which the parts are now secured by two

HULA KI'I: Hawaiian Puppetry

small metal nails, perhaps added in the Museum or by the collector. I should also like now to re-examine the neck, as well as the eyes.

The head, like the other separate heads, does not seem to have been a stick image of which the prop has either broken off or been cut off by a collector. Stick images were generally full figures (like the so-called Pele image). However, Buck (1957:483;484,Fig. 304c) describes a shark god, collected in 1825, with a broken-off prop (Bishop Museum No. 187) that he calls a "bodiless specimen" because it consists only of a human head with a short neck. It is curiously framed by a broken piece attached at the back that curves over the head and the face like a crest, with another part that is below the neck and curves forward and up like a scoop around the face.

Judging from the British Museum assembled puppet, the separate head Haw. 77 may have similarly been assembled with a torso and arms. The pasting of tapa on the wood further links the two. Sarah Stone's 1783 sketch of the head makes it certain that it is "traditional art" and that at the time of Cook's visit Hawaiians were already pasting tapa directly on wood and assembling images from parts. Such assembled images, at least as concerns the head, could be manipulated to make them seem alive.

Cox and Davenport (1974:193a), classifying Haw. 77 as a "fragment," think that "it was probably used with a torso and arms," as in the British Museum figure +249 they consider a temple image. They add, "Or it may have been the head of a marionette or puppet used in certain hula performances, as described by Emerson. . . ." They offer (p. 193b) the same explanation for the second separate British Museum head (Haw. 76).

4. British Museum Head (Haw. 76)

The second head (Haw. 76) also reached the Museum before 1880 as its type of number shows, and is listed as "Head of an idol" from the Sandwich Islands. Its history is less known than that of Haw. 77. The masculine face, more realistically carved than the other, is between 28 and 29 cm. high, and, according to

Museum Puppet Figures and Heads

Museum records, is made "of pale wood, blackened all over. The neck is elongated and appears to have been broken off. The eyes are formed of pearl shell, and the head is carved with tufts of small feathers about a half inch apart of which little but the roots remain. Around the temples there was formerly a line of tufts of human hair: of these only two are at all perfect." The head is now affixed to a display stand making it difficult to examine.

Some other existing images have tufts of hair doubled over and inserted into holes drilled in the wood, but none has both hair and feathers inserted in the same head. A possible exception may be a humanoid figure joining two bowls (British Museum Haw. 47) that has both human hair and a bundle of red feathers on its head. However, the attachment of the bundle is not explained (Cox and Davenport 1974:173).

The very narrow head (Haw. 76) has an egg-shaped face; a modelled nose; pronounced brow ridges; large, round, pearl-shell eyes pegged in and showing pupils; and a rather small open mouth with wooden teeth. The technique for inserting the teeth was not determined. Unlike the puppet and Haw. 77 this head has no helmet. The neck is thicker than that of the puppet but its considerable narrowing toward the end probably caused it to break off. Blackening the face may have been done to simulate dark skin—or to make it look like an antique to an early curio-collector. Still, pegging in hair and feathers on the head does not seem like a technique to undertake if meeting a customer's deadline. This head was, I think, produced within fifty years after Cook and may be conservatively classified as "evolved traditional art" since no documentation makes it part of the Cook collection.

5. The Missing Head

The present whereabouts of the third separate head (perhaps that of a puppet) from the Sandwich Islands to reach London is unknown. However, it definitely arrived on HMS *Blonde* in 1826 in the collection of either the Reverend Richard Rowland Bloxam, the Chaplain, or his younger brother, Andrew Bloxam, a naturalist. In 1826, this head and five other artifacts in the same collection were sketched and described by another brother, Matthew Holbeche Bloxam (1826:7). An unsigned, undated note, perhaps by M. H. Bloxam, written on a copy of the article in the Bishop Museum Manuscript Collection, states that the objects are "now in the possession of my mother and Rugby." The Bloxam brothers' family home was in Warwickshire, where their father, the Reverend Richard Rouse Bloxam, was one of the Masters of Rugby. Another note signed by "A. R. Bloxam" (Andrew Roby Bloxam, the naturalist's son) was written before July, 1922, and states: "I do not know at all what became of Nos. 1, 4 and 6 [No. 6 is the head]. They may presently be at the Rugby School Museum to which Mr. Matthew H. Bloxam gave a very large collection of antiquities and curios."

M. H. Bloxam states in his published article: "No. 6. Another wooden idol with a curiously shaped crest. This is covered with stripes of red, blue, and yellow cloth; the eyes are made of mother-of-pearl and in the mouth are two rows of teeth."

The engraving of the head depicts alternating light, intermediately colored, and dark stripes—nine of them on the crest, with the intermediately shaded stripes having a zigzag design. The cap, with seven alternating stripes of the same colors, extends over the forehead and around the sides of the face with no ears visible. The neck is round and has a broken terminal peg, probably inserted into a hollow torso to serve as the handle for the animator to grasp. Neither the neck nor its peg has any "cloth" (tapa) on it. The pearl-shell eyes appear to have pupils, which suggests the wooden-peg technique of insertion. The undescribed teeth, perhaps small shark teeth, seem set around the open mouth almost as if on the lips.

The head represents a chief with a helmet that looks like a variation of the wide-crested type. The base of the curved crest extends from just back of the top of the head to the neck. The crest itself, towering exceptionally high and wide, particularly in proportion to the size of the head, tapers to a point high above the somewhat realistically carved face.

The head is classifiable as "evolved traditional art," since it obviously follows forms similar to art collected on Cook's voyage.

Museum Puppet Figures and Heads

However, it was collected at a later time. Like Haw. 77 and the puppet it may have been assembled with a torso and arms as a manipulable figure.

Cox and Davenport (1974:192f) also think it was once part of an assembled figure. They suggest that it was "probably collected at Hale-o-Keawe, Honaunau, Hawaii, in 1825 by the Bloxam party. . . ." Research by Kaeppler (1978) documenting artifacts attributed to the Bloxams and others on the *Blonde* in 1825, and particularly those said to come from Hale-o-Keawe, a royal mausoleum, casts doubt on many attributions to this place.

Frequently these erroneous attributions arise from unawareness of the numerous artifacts the Bloxams, especially Richard, received as gifts, and others which they bought. Andrew Bloxam (1925:47) paid a dollar for "two very old and curious carved idols," and Richard Bloxam (1923:78) on one occasion received among other objects "curiously carved carvings . . . several wooden idols. . . ." Other crew members also obtained many curios, either old or newly made for them.

Hale-o-Keawe is so often cited as the source of the Bloxams' collections because they were among the few officers permitted by Prime Minister Kalanimoku to enter the mausoleum and remove images of gods and other objects. They were not permitted, however, to take effigies encasing the bones of the illustrious dead. The officers were the first foreigners to enter. Neither Captain Cook nor the Reverend William Ellis had been allowed inside. It was one of the few sacred enclosures undamaged during the 1819 revolution. Despite the great sorrow and dismay of the still faithful guardian, the party from the *Blonde* made a large collection but there is no evidence that the separate wooden head, now missing, was from the mausoleum. (A. Bloxam 1925: 74–76;R. R. Bloxam 1923:79–80;Byron 1826:201;Dampier 1971: 67–70.)

Among the offerings to the deified dead noted by the Bloxams were a Chinese mask and an English drum. The custom of making offerings—fish, tapa, and other native products as well as foreign artifacts—to win the favor of the spirits of the deified chiefs did not end with the 1819 revolution or the 1825 curio-collection.

HULA KI'I: Hawaiian Puppetry

In 1829 Dowager Queen Ka'ahumanu, now the leading Christian convert in the kingdom, entered Hale-o-Keawe to remove the bones of twenty-four members of royalty to bury them elsewhere. She found among the offerings an expensive and comparatively new foreign "object" that had been recently offered to the spirit of Kala'imamahu, half-brother of Kamehameha the Great. Chiefess Kekauluohi, his daughter who had been the wife of both Kamehameha the Great and Kamehameha II, had perhaps made the offerings as she was still not wholly committed to Christianity, and clung to some old customs (Bingham 1847:426).

6. Berlin Museum Head

A humanoid wooden head in Berlin Museum für Völkerkunde (VI 7269) was purchased in 1887 from Dr. Eduard Arning, Hamburg, who had been the leprosy specialist from 1884 to 1886 under Kalākaua, and who had collected over 600 Hawaiian artifacts and much tapa (Eichhorn 1929:3;Koch 1973:141,147). He obtained the head and a large "temple drum" from J. W. Pflüger, German Consul-General in Honolulu, who in 1881 had taken them from an "old heiau" in Wai'anae, O'ahu. A specialist on Hawaiian sculpture declared that the head was not even Hawaiian. However, it is most likely a post-European Hawaiian puppet head, for many details recall the separate heads and those of the ten puppets. Wai'anae, it will be recalled, was the home of Kukuhoi who taught puppetry to Pa'akaula at Moanalua. The drum and the head may have belonged to a hula master, as this type of drum *(ka'eke,* later called *pahu)* was used not only in heiaus but in dignified types of hula. *Hula ki'i* was rarely dignified.

A. Eichhorn (1929:Fig. 38;22–23) quotes Arning's notes as stating that the head is that of an idol and modern. Eichhorn adds that it is 34 cm. high and crudely carved from spongy, yellow wood. The head was not very old at the time collected because it is in relatively good condition. According to Eichhorn and my study of the artifact the head has a flat back; a broad, full face covered with grayish-white oil paint continued to just under the chin.

Museum Puppet Figures and Heads

Most of the round, log-like neck is unpainted. The face has a very prominent nose, modelled ears, slightly opened lips painted reddish-brown, a small mouth with two irregular rows of small teeth, narrow curved eyebrows colored black, and closely set oval eyes filled with pearl shell. The shell on the left is missing while that on the right, which was probably pasted into place, is round and partly fills the socket which has no pupil. The two rows of teeth, said by Eichhorn to be the palatine teeth of a species of "snake" (Schlangenart) may, I think, be from a *pūhi paha*, a vicious type of moray eel that lives in rocky shoals and will attack people. From ear to ear over the top of the head are four incisions, 1 cm. deep, for gluing in single tufts of dark brown human hair. Each tuft is up to 22 cm. long. There are three incisions over the occiput. Only the three more frontal furrows have had hair, and the most frontal one is reinforced by a wedge of linen cloth. The length and circumference of the round neck were not ascertained.

This most realistic of the separate wooden heads has an expressive face with rather a contemplative air, partly because of one missing shell eye which makes the other look like a monocle. Buck describes no images with hair glued in place but states (1957:469) that traditionally each tuft, doubled over, was wedged with tapa or wooden pegs to fit into a pit, rows of which extended across the head.

The Berlin head, mentioned neither by Buck nor Cox and Davenport, belongs to the same type of separate heads that were brought to England in that it too was probably assembled with a torso and arms to be manipulated. In other words, it would have been of the same structural type as the British Museum puppet. Other traditional elements shared with other existing examples of this type (and not with the nine puppets of the other type) are the teeth inserted into the mouth and the hair pegged into the head. All existing examples of both types (except the three in Bishop Museum) have pearl shell inserted either with paste or pegs into eye sockets. Nontraditional elements the Berlin head shares with the nine puppets in American museums are the greater realism and the use of foreign paint (gray like the National Museum pup-

HULA KI'I: Hawaiian Puppetry

pets and black on all puppets) as well as foreign cloth. The Berlin head represents modern "folk art" in its combination of traditional and nontraditional features.

The Berlin head with its eel-like teeth calls to mind a Wai'anae local legend told to McAllister (1933:117–119) during an archaeological survey near Mt. Kawiwi at the head of Wai'anae Valley. John Manini and Kaoanaeha Perry told him the origin of three meandering scars on the mountain side called Ka'onināpūhi, The Eel's Writhings. A couple living nearby had a beautiful thirty-year old daughter still a virgin because her parents thought no local man worthy of her. One day when mother and daughter had gone to the shore to fish they met a handsome stranger who helped them so much that they caught several mullet (*'anae*) and other fine fish instead of their usual small catch. This went on for some time until the stranger and the girl fell in love, and the parents, happy to have such a bountiful provider, let them marry. Twofold trouble began, first with jealous youths rumoring that the groom was a *kupua,* a supernatural being able to assume human form, and then with the bride's declining health.

Her brother, on going to Nanakuli to a famous kahuna, a priest skilled in diagnosis, learned that the husband was an eel-man who must be killed because he endangered the whole community's health. The parents, as suggested by the kahuna, confirmed the stranger's true nature while he slept, and saw eel-fins on his back. They and other villagers then plotted to kill him at a grand luau, a feast, to which they invited him.

When the warriors suddenly attacked him with their adzes, he turned into a fighting, writhing eel. They chopped off its head and threw it into the huge fire they had built at the foot of the mountain. Immediately the head flew back, joined the body, and kept on fighting. This happened many times, and the monster's writhings *(ka 'oni)* deeply scarred the mountain. The meandering grooves are now called Ka'onināpūhi. The warriors, at an old man's suggestion, finally killed the eel by laying their adzes over the severed body to prevent head and body from joining. They called the dead monster Pūhinalo, Obliterated Eel, and traced his

Museum Puppet Figures and Heads

origin to Pōhakuolapalapa in Pōka'ī Bay, Wai'anae. (See also Pukui, Elbert, Mookini 1974:86.) An eel who can take the form of a man and marry an unsuspecting woman is a frequent character, an obvious phallic symbol, in many Polynesian tales.

In 1886, valley residents would have been unimpressed had they seen "The Great Wizard of the North, Professor Anderson" at the Honolulu Opera House cut off his head and walk around with it under his arm (Frowe 1937:123–124). After all, their eel-man's head flew repeatedly back from the fire every time it was severed. The Wai'anae narrative makes me wonder if the Berlin head represents the mysterious stranger, the eel-man.

PART II
FUNCTIONS AND KINDS OF HULA KI'I

A. FUNCTIONS

The principal function of *hula ki'i,* like all hulas, was to entertain people of every social class and age either at private or public gatherings. *Hula ki'i,* whether by puppets or human imitators, was particularly intended to arouse laughter. Emerson (1909:94) states: "The songs that were cantillated to the hula ki'i express in some degree the peculiar libertinism of this [type of] hula, which differs from all others by many removes. They may be characterized as gossipy, sarcastic, ironical, scandal-mongering, dealing in satire, abuse, hitting right and left at social and personal vices— a cheese of rank flavor that is not to be partaken of too freely. It might be compared to the vaudeville in opera or to the genre picture in art."

Most, but not all, of the published puppetry meles (action-songs) satirize a man or a woman for deviation from customary behavioral norms, membership in a certain occupational group or social status, or pretensions of, or aspirations to, a higher social and political rank than judged to be warranted. Performers and audiences enjoyed personal and social freedom to ventilate shared feelings about certain individuals or types of personality in Hawaiian and local foreign society, and to make playfully but bitingly known the public's attitude toward them. By means of humor and insouciance the composers of *hula ki'i* meles and skits violated everyday restraints on speech and behavior and delighted in vicarious defiance of them. After all, the puppets were only wooden figures behaving outrageously, and not real people.

In dramatic skits a puppeteer's selection and exaggeration of salient traits of character and behavior brought laughter based on recognition and appreciation of his art and the nonhuman bodies of his inanimate figures. Distortion made ridiculous or comical not only villainy but heroism and coquetry. If a listener objected to certain words or gestures he was told he was injecting his own evil or foreign puritanical interpretations into the usually metaphorical language of the mele.

Verbal devices, not a puppet's physical appearance, cloth-

HULA KI'I: Hawaiian Puppetry

ing, or props, were the puppeteer's—or his drummer-chanter's—major resource, since the little images had limited flexibility. Hula people on the whole were very adept at shifty or secret talk, "a method," Emerson (p. 97) remarks, "of concealing one's meaning from all but the initiated, of which the Hawaiian, whether alii [chief] or commoner, was very fond," and which gave "appropriate flavor and gusto" to hula. In the highly verbal Hawaiian society entire families who specialized for generations in formal and informal contests of wit often played for high stakes. Aristocrats prided themselves on their manipulation of language, knowledge of traditions and genealogies, and talent in composition.

Experts could not translate certain puppetry meles because, they said, the words were unfamiliar "classical Hawaiian." Labelling them "unadulterated slang," Emerson (pp. 96–98), being well-versed in the language, surely recognized his informants' evasions in translating meles with sexual innuendos, but the evasions conveniently excused him from publishing other than free and inoffensive translations of such songs. He, apparently, did not object to the songs, dances, or myths, for he states (p. 12) that when these "children of passion, sensuous, worshipful of whatever lends to pleasure . . . do step into the mud it is not to tarry and wallow in it; it is rather with the unconscious naiveté of a child thinking no evil." His brother, the Reverend Oliver P. Emerson, would probably not agree. N. B. Emerson recommends that "if one's virtue will not endure the love-making of Arcadia, let him banish the myth from his imagination and hie to a convent or a nunnery" (p. 8).

Nonetheless, not all the "euphuistic stumbling blocks" he mentions arise from hidden ribald, critical, or hostile meanings. An occasional *ki'i* mele flatters a person with sentimental and nostalgic references to places and features of landscape or weather that symbolize sexual love and parts of the beloved person's body, or it covertly describes rising passion with bombastic and classical allusions to deeds and divine origin of the honored couple's ancestors. But even these meles accompanied by a puppet's lively but stilted motions or a human being's imitations probably made the audience smile with delight and appreciation.

Functions and Kinds of Hula Ki'i

Did *hula ki'i* ever have a religious function? Four reasons lead to the question. First, the Moanalua puppets, according to G. M. Damon, were "sacred," and people were afraid to touch them. Secondly, one or perhaps more of the detached wooden heads, probably of puppets, came from heiaus. Thirdly, the two images sketched in 1816 by Choris (1822:Plate V) at the 'Ahu'ena Heiau, Hawai'i, appear to have flexible arms like puppets which suggests they may have been used as puppets. Fourthly, many writers claim that hula originated as a men's religious dance in a temple service. They add that by the late eighteenth century the hula had become a secular, theatrical, and professional performance by both sexes. And that by the nineteenth century it had degenerated aesthetically and morally because of its pandering to foreign tastes and the irresponsible freedom that followed the 1819 overthrow of the taboo system. These writers include Emerson (1909: 7,11–13), Handy (1927:309;1931:12,29), Withington (1937:268), Pollenz (1948;1950), Costa (1951:111), and the Hawaii Visitors Bureau.

A general answer to the points raised is that every type of hula and its equipment were as sacred and as much associated with religion as, say, canoe-building and its tools, because religion penetrated every phase of life before 1819; a pantheon of gods and lesser spirits by means of a system of taboos controlled man and nature, which were inseparable; and each occupation had its priestly experts, kahunas, as well as its special shrines and heiaus dedicated to the gods who had originated and regulated it. When the "free-eaters" toppled this elaborate system of taboos in 1819, the religion crumbled. It did not completely vanish, however, for vestiges linger on today.

Nineteenth-century laws against kahunaism and Hawaiian religiously-based schools to teach hula and other traditional occupational knowledge did not prevent their continuation in secret. For hula schools *(hula hālau)* Emerson's description (1909:14–56) has become the modern standard although schools differed from each other (cf. Beamer 1976;Barrère,Pukui,Kelly 1980). Male and female students lived until after graduation in a school that had an altar to Hi'iaka, Kapo, Laka, the four Maile sisters, and other

HULA KI'I: Hawaiian Puppetry

supernatural originators, patrons, or teachers to whom students offered prayers each day and for whom they ritually gathered flowers and greenery. Students, separated from ordinary life, lived under a supernaturally sanctioned discipline while they learned not only dances, chants, and instrumental accompaniments, but prayers, rites, and myths. The most able became hula masters.

Like other priestly specialists, Pa'akaula, the Moanalua hula master-puppeteer, was probably inspired and protected by his hula gods who rewarded his devotion and punished any neglect or irreverence. To prevent his puppets and other hula equipment from spiritual defilement, physical damage, and betrayal of secrets he doubtless tabooed them to have the hula deities punish violations and keep people afraid to touch his things.

Unanswered questions about the separate wooden head found in 1881 in a Wai'anae heiau include: What is the name of the heiau and its function? Who deposited the head there? Was it the puppeteer or someone who knew that anything dedicated to the hula gods must be ritually disposed of to prevent their defilement? A puppet might make people uneasy; its seeming life comes from its animator who appears to transfer his spirit into it through his hands, voice, mind, and heart until the two are one. And the puppet's head, as the seat of mana, supernatural power, would be an especially sensitive part of the image. Hula students were taught to gather all discarded articles at the end of a day to deposit them ritually at a hula shrine or heiau; the same was done with everything discarded at the graduation ceremonies sometimes held at a hula heiau (Pukui 1980:76). The Reverend Hiram Bingham (1847), of the first company of missionaries to the islands, deplored the actions of dancers whom he saw leaving their faded wreaths as offerings at a hula shrine.

Claims that hula originated as religious service in a heiau with only men as performers are undocumented according to Barrère (1980:13–15), who examined descriptions of prehistoric and early historic hula by eighteenth-century foreigners and early nineteenth-century Hawaiian scholars. No evidence suggests that anciently only men did the hula; in fact the earliest written account, dated 1778, tells of women as well as men of various ages danc-

Functions and Kinds of Hula Ki'i

ing; and orally transmitted myths and legends name goddesses as creators, performers, and teachers of hula. There is no evidence either that hula "was performed as a religious rite within the precincts of any other type of heiau" than a hula heiau, but dance-gestures might enhance a rite.

The unsupported claims derive, directly or indirectly, mainly from N. B. Emerson's *Unwritten Literature of Hawaii* (1909) and to some extent from Curt Sachs' *World History of Dance* (1937). I shall deal here only briefly with the social evolutionary theories expressed in these classics. Both are serious studies of dance, and although written in a romantic, stimulating, and highly readable style present valuable factual data, which in Emerson's case had not been published previously.

Sachs' chronology of the evolution of world dance from the Proto-Paleolithic (and a backward glance at the apes) to the late Neolithic (and a forward look at the present) is adapted from Oswald Menghin's *Weltgeschichte der Steinzeit* (World History of the Stone Age), published in 1931. According to Menghin, a follower of the German-Austrian "Culture-Historical School," Polynesia and certain other areas of the world had attained by the time of first Western contact what he calls a Seignorial Culture *(Herrenkultur)*, a developmental stage in the Neolithic Late Tribal era. Sachs characterizes the Late Tribal dances as libido dances by mixed couples or individuals, with "a strong accent on the sexual . . ." and, "in their transition from the purely devotional and social to the professional and theatrical, these dances take for granted the division of labor and the class distinctions of an aristocratic and urban culture, which demands and supports the formation of a paid dancing profession for entertainment and public performance" (1937:215–217). Costa (1951:111ff.), who quotes Sachs on the matter of transition, also follows his lead in classifying types of dance and their social and material components in her survey of descriptions of dance in the Society and the Hawaiian Islands during the first seventy-five years of Western contact.

Sachs' characterization, necessarily broad to cover all Neolithic cultures of the type he and Menghin label Seignorial, needs modification to fit the Hawaiian. No documentary evidence supports the transition he describes for the dance. By 1778 the devotional, social, professional, and theatrical elements were inseparably combined. The successful exploitation of abundant marine and land resources in fishing and horticulture had produced a large population but no urbanization. The class structure was almost caste-like, particularly in regard to the highest class consisting of persons who traced their descent from gods. There was much division of labor with specialists who had undergone technological and religious training for their work. Among the specialists were troupes of entertainers who hoped to find a generous and wealthy chief as a patron. Upper-class members also performed publicly and privately. Sexuality was both explicit and implicit in many dances and chants, and was most explicit during socially approved periods of completely uninhibited expression of emotion, as during mourning over a highborn person's death or during the annual harvest celebration, the Makahiki, which lasted three or four months. The celebration honored Lono, one of the gods of fertility in nature and man, and solemn ceremonies were followed by feasts, sports, games, dancing, and other entertainment. The joyous period was religious in the sense that the activities were under the patronage not only of Lono but the gods and goddesses who had originated and supported them.

Emerson, unlike Sachs, states no specific source for his fragile evolutionary chronology, which is basically a reflection of his broadly humanistic views on social evolution. Like Sachs, but only incidentally, he takes into account the migration of peoples and diffusion of cultural elements. Hula ki'i to Emerson (1909:91) is an indigenous art, not one introduced by Europeans or Americans, but a probable part of the cultural heritage Hawaiians brought from their ancestral home in the south Pacific or ultimately Asia. Costa (1951) quotes Pukui as doubting Emerson's theory that Hawaiian puppetry is pre-European because she found no old Hawaiian dancers and hula masters who knew of it before Pa'akaula's. Obviously they were unfamiliar with Kaumuali'i's puppets on Kaua'i in 1820.

To Emerson, Hawaiians in 1778 were at a cultural level through which "our Anglo-Saxon ancestors" had already passed. He

Functions and Kinds of Hula Ki'i

hoped his book would make the "Anglo-Saxon mind" appreciate the hula as it was before vulgar European tastes had contaminated it. Nonetheless, he also discusses new hulas and songs created well into Kalākaua's reign. Attempts to suppress all hula did not please N. B. Emerson who idealistically describes hula "of the olden time" (undefined); his brother Oliver P. Emerson (1928:209–210) felt not enough was done to eliminate this "evil."

However, N. B. Emerson's over-enthusiastic defense of "ancient" hula leads to such unsupported, extreme, and misleading statements (1909:13) as: "The ancient Hawaiians did not personally and informally indulge in the dance for their own amusement . . . [they] left it to be done for them by a body of trained and paid performers . . . because [it required] special education and arduous training . . . and more especially because it was a religious matter, to be guarded against profanation by the observance of tabus and the performance of priestly rites."

This and similarly broadly phrased statements ignoring the rest of the culture are the major source of other writers' unqualified and unsupported statements about hula as sacred. Yet Emerson surely knew that other occupations had their special gods, heiaus, and rituals to sanctify their equipment and work, for he was born and raised in the Islands, spent most of his life there, and as a child knew Hewahewa, a former high priest and a leader in the 1819 revolution. Oddly enough, Emerson does not mention the existence of special heiaus and shrines for hula but focuses on the ritualized and supernaturally sanctioned training and performance in hula schools equipped with altars to deities of the dance.

He nowhere states that men were the first dancers. That notion and the claim that hula was originally only a temple service by men comes principally from later writers who elaborate on their knowledge that women, with very rare exceptions, were indeed excluded from certain types of heiaus because men believed their presence would defile the place.

If the two puppet-like images standing at 'Ahu'ena Heiau, Hawai'i, outside the tabooed area enclosed in palisades, were manipulated as puppets, they were not sacred. Kamakau (1961:

HULA KI'I: Hawaiian Puppetry

203), who discusses these unconsecrated images, adds that "at times they were used by the people who kept the houses of the gods to fire the cook ovens," and were set up "for decoration to make the god house handsome and attractive to the god when he came from heaven." He calls these decorative images *keiki pu'ipu'i* ("chubby children" is one translation). If the sculptor indeed made the two images' arms manipulable like those of existing puppets his intent may have been to create a novelty to welcome and amuse the god on his arrival.

The Hawaiian puppets and their activities, whether dancing a hula, acting in a play, or perhaps ornamenting a heiau, are sacred only in the holistic sense that they and their animators had their place in the religious network that tightly united the Hawaiian world before 1819; but within that network, as Kamakau makes clear, there was no contradiction in identifying some things as sacred *(kapu)* and others as common, non-sacred *(noa)* according to a specific situation, time, or individual. In this narrower sense the manipulable figures were *noa* except when an individual of sufficient rank, mana, or supernatural training chose to make them otherwise.

B. KINDS OF HULA KI'I

1. Introduction

Records seldom clarify the kind, or combination of kinds, of *hula ki'i;* the number of wooden or live performers; or the occasion for any given performance. Emerson, for instance, after discussing puppet dramas and entr'actes, quotes six *hula ki'i* meles without telling, except for one danced by his informant, whether puppets or people, or both, performed them.

With the arbitrary criterion of whether or not a performance takes place behind a screen I tentatively distinguish seven kinds of *hula ki'i.* Few are distinctive enough to be called types, and more than one kind may combine or overlap with another in an actual performance. When a screen is used, puppets are the stars; when there is no screen, human dancers are, but if a puppet is present it may steal the show. In *hula ki'i* with a screen, puppets perform behind it to (1) dance, (2) act in dramatic skits or plays, or (3) act or dance at the same time as people who perform either in front of or behind the screen. In *hula ki'i* without a screen, human dancers (4) imitate absent puppets, (5) imitate puppets either absent or present on the open stage, (6) wear puppets as body masks, or (7) dance while a puppet acts on the stage with them.

These kinds of *hula ki'i* are reported up to the early twentieth century after which published references to the art are rare. However, a few Hawaiians have kept one kind or another in their repertoires and developed new types combining Hawaiian and foreign features in structure and performance.

2. Theatrics

With supplementary notes from traditional hula custom, the following scanty data from examples of the kinds of *hula ki'i* to be presented later suggest the existence of a theatrical pattern.

A puppeteer's tapa screen (later one of foreign cloth) is long and wide enough to conceal one or more manipulators, who,

HULA KI'I: Hawaiian Puppetry

according to Emerson (1909:92), stand. That a puppeteer ever sat or kneeled while working is not mentioned. No backdrops are mentioned or any control of access to the puppeteers' area except perhaps through taboos which prevent meddling. Not reported is how a puppeteer arranges his figures to have them ready to perform, or in what, if anything, he transports and stores them between performances.

Tapa or foreign cloth in styles like those worn by pre- and post-European Hawaiian nobility clothes the puppets and hides the animator's hands. In one structural type of puppet, it will be recalled, he can move both the head and arms by inserting his hand inside the hollow torso. In the other type only the arms are movable and are manipulated from outside the torso. Weapons, the only props mentioned, presumably were tied to the warrior's hands. Several of the puppets and separate heads in museums represent chiefs, some with fixed helmets. When human performers imitate puppets in front of, or sometimes behind, the screen they wear whatever the current fashion is in ornaments and costumes for dancers or spectators.

A puppeteer learns the art as a student in hula school or after graduation from a relative or friend who may give him his first puppets. Information about the carvers is scanty. That more men than women are mentioned among nineteenth-century puppeteers may or may not be significant. During the last half-century women as well as men have been performing with puppets or dancing like them; children of both sexes are among performers. If several puppets perform at the same time behind a screen each animator handles two. However, a puppeteer can work alone if he has only two images active while the others watch.

Performances continued to be sponsored through the nineteenth century and sometimes later by wealthy nobles of the community for guests of their own social class. They provided performers with the basic remuneration but spectators threw gifts to them as a supplement. In earlier times the dancers received Hawaiian gifts of all kinds suitable to their rank and needs, and in post-European times, money and foreign objects were given. Until the end of the monarchy the most able hula masters

Functions and Kinds of Hula Ki'i

worked at courts of chiefs and kings and sometimes passed on the position with their equipment and secrets to qualified relatives. It is unknown whether any of the many strolling entertainers without fixed affiliations included puppetry among their arts.

Traditionally, when puppets dance and act behind a screen the lower border is on a level with the invited spectators seated on mats on the floor in front of it. The place may be a private residence or a longhouse *(hālau)*. If the latter has been built for a hula school it has an altar to hula gods, and a public program there will observe more taboos and rites to honor the deities than a performance elsewhere. Many programs are held out-of-doors in a cleared area, with honored guests seated nearest the dance area and others, commoners, standing behind them or perched in trees. Nowadays in outdoor programs a stage is often raised above the audience seated on the grass in chairs. One wonders if in Honolulu in 1821 a stage was raised, not for performers, but for Kamehameha II and his guests to watch hundreds of men, women, and children dancing out-of-doors in a hula marathon that included *hula ki'i* to honor him.

Hula ki'i was also on the program in the Opera House and in a specially built structure during Kalākaua's reign. On an evening in 1886 the six royal puppets did the hula in the Opera House on the King's birthday; the manipulator, presumably a royal hula master, was invisible behind a screen on the stage while invited guests sat on chairs below. Three years earlier the King had an official eight-hour-long hula program that included human imitators of puppets in a temporary amphitheater constructed on the Palace grounds that seated about 4,000 spectators, mostly Hawaiians. Many, it seems, sat on the ground, getting so close to the dancers as to leave them little room. Outside as many or more people tried to see the show.

Traditionally, programs were held in daylight hours, preferably in the cool of morning or late afternoon, but when they continued into the night either the moon or torches provided light. Some of Kalākaua's programs had electric light.

Sound for *hula ki'i* consists traditionally of the human voice, the double-gourd drum, or both. There is no report of ventrilo-

HULA KI'I: Hawaiian Puppetry

quism, mechanical vocal devices, or a special tone or style of speech to distinguish wooden from live performers. Either the puppeteer or the principal drummer-chanter (if there is more than one) speaks or chants. In a play or in a dialogue with a spectator or the instrumentalist, the puppeteer, of course, voices the words supposedly spoken by the puppets. Human dancers imitating puppets or performing with them join in to chant all or part of a song, or to mouth the words silently. The musician, male or female, is often the senior and most experienced member, a hula master, who knows the meles, gives the beat, explains the song or story to the audience, and acts as interlocutor for the puppets' pantomime or talk.

The large double-gourd drum *(ipu hula* or *pā hula)* is made of two hollow gourds *(ipu, Lagenaria siceraria)* of unequal size—the lower large and long, the upper small and round—sewn or glued together, with a suspensory cord of tapa or other material around the join (Buck 1957:405–407;406,Fig. 264). The drummer, kneeling or sitting on the floor to one side of the audience and performers, holds the cords with one hand in order to raise and thump the drum on the floor mat or his knee, while with the other he slaps or taps the drum or lifts it to make gestures illustrating the song. What he does in a puppet performance depends, of course, on whether the song or action is vigorous or gentle in spirit. Some spectators consider the musician more important than the dancers in making a program a success.

The construction of a Hawaiian puppet does not prevent it from effectively and amusingly mimicking a hula, for the basic hula movements emphasize motions of arms and hips rather than of feet. A dancer, whether alone or in an ensemble, does not take continuously proceeding steps but does return steps of two or three steps forward and back or sideways, or even stands in one place moving the heels up and down. The number of basic hip movements is limited and can be simulated by moving the puppets' garments. They can broadly imitate conventional arm, but not finger, gestures to signify love, cold, sea, canoe, precipice, rain, and the like. The Moanalua puppets' wooden arms can mimic only larger arm movements, up, down, and across, where-

Functions and Kinds of Hula Ki'i

as the royal puppets, having more flexible arms, have a wider range. Puppets made with separate heads can be turned so that their glistening pearl-shell eyes seem to follow their hand and arm motions; the long slender neck inside the hollow torso is a kind of control rod, long enough to make the head easy to move while the arm-strings are also being manipulated.

For an important event, a hula master plans a program according to his specialties, preferences, and, most importantly, the occasion. If a highborn person is to be honored with a program of many types of hula, the organizer customarily starts with the more serious, slower chants and dances that praise the person and his ancestry, and goes on to the more light-hearted, gay, rapid types like *hula ki'i* and *hula ma'i* (genitals hula), which may be combined when a human dancer uses a puppet to illustrate the *mele ma'i* that celebrates the vigor and successes of the person's sexual parts upon which the continuation of the ancestral line depends. If the sequence of hula types and songs in the program expresses an inner meaning or tells a story based on myth or tradition, the *hula ki'i* fits in wherever its meles will carry out the underlying central theme. No information exists on how skits and plays (most likely the hula master's compositions or adaptations) fit into a program. At informal social gatherings an impromptu program that may include puppet imitations is organized around a theme chosen by the ranking person or someone who chooses a flattering topic. Guests then compose new chants or revise old ones to accord with the theme, and perform them.

Traditional hula training emphasizes memory, but reading and writing—missionary-taught skills highly valued even by Hawaiians who rejected foreign religion—spurred the writing down of chants; some were published in Hawaiian-language newspapers but several families are known to still have notebooks filled with unpublished variants. That a literate hula master wrote down any or all of his most important programs is undocumented, but the most celebrated written and printed hula program is that for King Kalākaua's belated coronation. The King himself, being exceptionally musically gifted, selected over 260 items and arranged them in groups, each under the name of one of seven hula mas-

HULA KI'I: Hawaiian Puppetry

ters in charge of a group. The third of the groups listed has *hula ki'i* at the end of that hula master's assignment, as will be discussed later; this type does not appear in the other six groups. The pattern for the program as a whole and for each group remains to be analyzed, but, in general, the central theme is the glorification of Kalākaua himself, Queen Kapi'olani, their ancestors, and their crowns (the first worn by Hawaiian royalty). However, toward the end of the eight-hour program the King listed a series of dances done to selections from the epic-like cycle of chants, sacred to hula people, about Pele, her youngest sister Hi'iaka, and Pele's lover Lohi'au whom she sent Hi'iaka to Kaua'i to fetch for her (cf. Barrère, Pukui, Kelly 1980; their Appendix D, 133–139, has a reproduction of the original program).

C. HULA KI'I WITH A SCREEN

1. Puppets as Dancers

Two accounts, one dated 1820, the other 1886, describe puppets doing the hula behind their screen for royalty and their guests.

As noted previously, the earliest reference to puppetry states that in 1820 at Waimea, Kaua'i, six puppets ("idols" in a secular sense) danced a hula ("hoory hoory") behind a screen of tapa ("tappers"). King Kaumuali'i and Queen Kapule (who were still somewhat independent of King Kamehameha the Great) had invited the missionaries, Mr. and Mrs. Samuel Whitney and Mr. and Mrs. Samuel Ruggles, who had arrived at their new station on July 25, to visit them at their residence during the afternoon of July 29, 1820. Later that day Mrs. Mercy Whitney wrote in her journal (E. Damon 1925:208):

> We went, & found them sitting on a mat, surrounded by a numerous train. We soon learned they were going to have a hoory hoory (Idol dance) for amusement. A curtain of tappers was fitted across the room & soon after we entered, an old man began to make noise by drumming on a hollow instrument with his hands, & at the same time singing. After singing & drumming some time, six idols made their appearance above the curtain, & began to dance. Their motion was regular with the music. We were soon convinced of the folly & vanity of such an exhibition, & as soon as politeness would permit, took leave of the King & Queen and returned home.

In the diary she wrote for her parents, Nancy Ruggles, who also deplored "the vanities of the heathen" exhibited that afternoon, gives no clue as to the nature of the "plays" seen. The King's gifts of food and shelter were acceptable but not the en-

HULA KI'I: Hawaiian Puppetry

tertainment by which he also wished to please them (Ruggles 1924:656):

> July 29th. This afternoon the King exhibited a scene of plays, gave us an invitation, to which we did not readily comply; sent the second time, accordingly we went. I don't know when I have had my mind more impressed with the vanities of the heathen than I had in witnessing this scene. O when will this untutored tribe sit down at our Immanuel's feet, and receive the benign influences of the Gospel.
>
> Nancy R.

Sixty-six years later, on the evening of November 18, 1886, at the Opera House (also called Music Hall), Honolulu, a large and "distinguished audience" (present by royal invitation) did not consider the dancing of six royal puppets "folly & vanity" but demanded an encore. In perhaps their first and only public performance outside royal residences, the puppets stole the show when they did a hula as an entr'acte after the second tableau in "the long talked of" four-act "Historical Tableaux" based on the life of Kamehameha the Great. The amused and delighted audience, finding the puppets a refreshing novelty after the serious "Tableaux," demanded that they repeat their hula. The occasion was one of numerous events King Kalākaua had scheduled for the two-week-long Golden Jubilee to celebrate his fiftieth birthday (Frowe 1937.129 ff.).

According to the *Pacific Commercial Advertiser* (Nov. 29, 1886, quoted by Frowe 1937:130):

> ... the exhibit of the ancient 'Punch and Judy' of the Hawaiians created much amusement and it had to be repeated. When the curtain went up a Hawaiian woman was seen squatting on the stage, beating a 'hula paipu' and chanting meles. Behind her was a screen, some six feet in length. At a given time six small figures, dressed in Hawaiian costume, appeared above the top of the screen and went

Functions and Kinds of Hula Ki'i

through a series of antics, keeping time with the beat of the paipu.

A Hawaiian-language newspaper reported that when the six puppets (*po'e hula ki'i, hula ki'i* folk) appeared and a woman, who beat an *ipu,* began to sing the puppets were made to dance (*ha'a),* which created "shouts of laughter and great commotion" (*Ka Nupepa Kuokoa,* Dec. 4,1886;trans. Barrère 1980:55). One of the more specific meanings of *ha'a* is "the bent-knee hula." I find no information about the mele to which the puppets danced or the names of the puppeteer and the drummer. The official printed program lists the "Tableaux" but none of the hulas, not even that of the puppets.

The newspapers' favorable report on the puppets' hula is not mentioned in histories written by Kalākaua's opponents. Alexander (1896:16–17), remarking that the "night was made hideous" by the hula drum and the conch in the Palace yard as kahunas assembled from other islands to prepare for the celebration, commented that a "hulahula dance" concluded the Opera House program and "gave offense to most of the audience." He does not mention puppets; perhaps the offensive dances (probably *hula ma'i)* were by live dancers. Another severe critic (Thurston 1936:23) tells of "hulas, of more than questionable character, which had long been interdicted by the government . . . [being] frequently displayed at evening in the Palace grounds" during the long celebration.

The King's decision to display the royal puppets resulted, I conjecture, not only from his revival and frequent reinterpretation of traditional customs, especially hula, but from the sensational success a few months earlier when, in two engagements a month apart at the Opera House, "the world's monarch ventriloquist," Fred W. Millis, and his "Six Merry Manikins," provided "unique Millis entertainment, *Sans Souci,* and humorous sketches." (Quotations about Millis from the *Advertiser,* March 16,18,19,22,23, April 6,1886; cited by Frowe 1987:122–123, with titles of some songs and plays performed.)

HULA KI'I: Hawaiian Puppetry

In his first engagement in Honolulu, after arriving from Australia in March, Millis had a "good audience" and with the the aid of his six manikins—Chinese, Irish, Yankee, Dutch, Negro, and "a maiden-of-uncertain-age"—as well as with a "rapid change of voice made local hits which fairly brought down the house." When the Chinese manikin began to sing, "six Chinese in the audience and those in the gallery jumped up from their seats and made a laughable exit, causing much amusement." A special matinee with special numbers was requested; and seated in "the largest afternoon audience ever in this city" were the king's sisters, Princesses Lili'uokalani and Likelike, and the latter's eleven-year-old daughter, Princess Ka'iulani.

When Millis returned in April from a succcessful tour of Maui and Hawai'i, the Opera House again drew large crowds, with the Six Merry Manikins again receiving special mention: "The hour with 6 manikins was much enjoyed. He was compelled to sing that Lardy-dah again." For his "final great benefit" before leaving the islands, Millis arranged "a monster programme."

Both young and old, the *Advertiser* declares, had enjoyed the performances, most of all those of the Six Merry Manikins; and to the audiences, which were not only large but "quite select and inclined to be critical," Millis as a ventriloquist surpassed even "the great and celebrated Maccabe." In 1883, Maccabe had received very favorable notices, although before his arrival it had been expected that he would prove a disappointment because he was "a clean-shaven ventriloquist, without puppets." There is no word on whether Millis, a ventriloquist with puppets, had the requisite beard!

I find no answer to the inevitable question of how it happens that the Kaumuali'i, Kalākaua, Millis, and Moanalua puppeteers each had a troupe of *six* puppets.

As the reference to beardless, puppetless Maccabe implies, Millis was not the first to present a foreign puppetry troupe in the islands and pave the way for the enthusiastic reception given to the local puppets. In earlier years, at least two other famous troupes of wooden manikins, or minstrels as they were often called, had performed. Although they were not as enthusiastically

Functions and Kinds of Hula Ki'i

received as Millis, they probably created interest in seeing good puppetry performances.

Early in December, 1874, John E. McDonough's Royal Marionettes with "the original Prof. Rice's Wooden Minstrels" arrived in Honolulu "unsolicited" (*Advertiser,* Dec.5,1874; Frowe 1937: 12). Perhaps the decision to secure a Honolulu engagement was not made until the ship carrying the company on a Southern Hemisphere tour lay over for a couple of days. Typically the variety acts encompassed "spectacular dramas" ["Babes in the Wood," with appropriate music, and "Charm of the Household"], the famous Barnum Box trick, and aerial suspension tableaux, but the company's performances at the Royal Hawaiian Theatre were scarcely mentioned in the newspapers. McDonough, former American manager of the English company of The Royal Marionettes, had started his own company of the same name, and had combined forces with "Professor Rice," a mind reader and puppeteer (cf. McPharlin 1969:179,188).

Walter E. Deaves, one of McDonough's puppeteers who had not joined the Pacific tour but who had quit and established his own marionette company called Deaves Marvelous Manikins, arrived in Honolulu in early August, 1884, for a week-long stay. According to McPharlin (1969:268), Deaves "presented an entertainment built around the puppet show, playing in the chief settlements and even in the palace of Queen Liliuokalani [she was still only a princess]. The puppet numbers were *Cinderella,* a minstrel show, and an olio of variety in the Royal Marionette tradition." In 1884, Honolulu also saw a marionette show of "Humpty Dumpty" (Frowe 1937:170). As Deaves had a harlequinade-inspired skit of that name (McPharlin 1969:272–273), I assume it was also on his Honolulu program.

Before the Deaves company had arrived from San Francisco on the *Mariposa,* a local newspaper had anticipated "some fun," but the minstrelsy and other variety acts and the three-foot-high string-operated marionettes drew few people to the evening performance ("a calabash would have covered them"); however, the children's matinees were well attended. The newspaper concluded that Deaves Marvelous Manikins had come to Honolulu

HULA KI'I: Hawaiian Puppetry

"at an unfortunate time and after their first performance the best plan would have been to have visited the other islands" (*Bulletin*, Aug.18,29,1884;Frowe 1937:85). On his return to the United States, Deaves formed the "Deaves Royal Marionettes" with his brother Harry, but he later replaced the Royal Marionette formula with a show-within-a-show format in which puppet spectators imitated the real audience. Walter Deaves, who created numerous other innovations, went on to extraordinary success on his equally extraordinarily extensive world travels, including an engagement in Honolulu in 1912 (McPharlin 1969:268–271). Perhaps this 1912 visit decided the Damons to have Pa'akaula and his fellow puppeteers at Moanalua exhibit local Hawaiian puppetry to W. A. Bryan of Bishop Museum who visited them about this time. There is no doubt that these famous foreign troupes inspired Hawaiian pride and interest in their own local puppets and may have helped expand the puppets' repertoires.

Surely the foreign puppetry troupes in 1874, 1884, and especially in 1886 influenced Kalākaua's decision to display his own royally sponsored troupe. England had its Royal Marionettes; the Hawaiian Islands had its Royal *Hula Ki'i!* Although the King's many enemies never let anyone forget that he was not of the Kamehameha line and had attained the throne by a bitterly and violently contested election in 1874, he enjoyed his membership in the exclusive "clan" of world royalty. On his round-the-world tour in 1881, the first by any monarch, he had been welcomed by members of the royal "clan" in Asia and Europe as an affable, personable, and highborn royal kinsman. Impressed by their courts and trappings of state, this superb showman on his return united many elements of the grand foreign royal subculture with elements from the local Hawaiian culture in his two major public ceremonies and celebrations—his belated coronation in 1883 and his birthday Jubilee in 1886. He loved the theater and knew much about it, and planned the celebrations as great shows. One of his most successful ideas was to have his royal hula master exhibit the six royal puppets in the familiar Hawaiian theatrical pattern and doing a Hawaiian dance. The public acclaim proba-

Functions and Kinds of Hula Ki'i

bly brought into the open other puppet troupes that had been performing in secret and emboldened new imitations.

2. Puppet Plays

"The hula ki'i was, perhaps, the nearest approximation made by the Hawaiians to a genuine dramatic performance," states Emerson (1909:92) in describing "a sample of the stories illustrated." Emerson's is the only documentary evidence of any Hawaiian prehistoric or early historic prose drama for either living or wooden actors. None is mentioned by eighteenth-century explorers who saw many prose plays and skits in central Polynesia (Luomala 1979). Connecting parts of a program with a story-telling theme is rarer and simpler in the northern islands than in the central area. Hawaiians, it seems, still prefer poems, sometimes with dialogue, acted out in dances accompanied by chanting and instruments; a few meles have an overt story line but most draw on metaphors, especially those based on natural phenomena, and cryptic allusions to express thoughts and feelings about people and events. That Hawaiians classify prose puppet plays as a type of hula may point to the concept of drama as a later development than that of dance.

Apparently James Beattie's Honolulu productions like his "Oscar and Malvina" (Campbell 1822:148-149) in 1809 did not turn any Hawaiian toward creating prose plays, and the unnamed informant who told Theodore-Adolphe Barrot, a French consul visiting from Manila, about Hawaiian plays may have had Beattie's play in mind in which a Hawaiian chiefess took the leading role. Barrot (1850:33-34), after attending a hula program in 1836 at the Nu'uanu Valley home of Kamehameha III, quotes his informant as follows: "Many females, even of the royal family, had the reputation of being finished actresses, for this people once had plays, and the members only of distinguished families appeared upon the stage."

Records after 1809 report no stimulus for prose drama with either foreign or native themes and actors. In 1825 the officers of

HULA KI'I: Hawaiian Puppetry

the HMS *Blonde* performed no plays in the islands although they joined with officers of other English ships they met in South America on the return journey to put on a play and an afterpiece on shore. In 1832 the "Thespian Corps" of the U.S. Frigate *Potomac* played a tragic piece and a comic afterpiece for Kamehameha III at his palace on a Saturday afternoon, which displeased the missionaries and their more zealous converts as it interfered with preparations for the Sabbath. Two years later, a newly arrived couple interested in drama got a few young foreign and Hawaiian members of the Honolulu social set to form an amateur theatrical society to play farces and scenes from Shakespeare, but there was nothing original or with a Hawaiian subject. The King offered the use of his palace for the first performance and acted as stage manager. When even Thursday-evening scheduling did not prevent criticism of the entertainment as frivolous and the King's participation as improper, the site was changed to Major Warren's Hotel. After the two organizers left the islands, the remaining members were unsuccessful in carrying on by themselves (Hoyt 1961:12–14).

During the reign of Kamehameha III, it will be recalled, his hula master acquired the six puppets now in the National Museum. It was from his younger brother that Emerson learned about the puppet plays. His "sample," "one of the different hula-plays of the hula ki'i," is a comedy and the only native Hawaiian drama reported except for Kalākaua's "Historical Tableaux" at the Opera House in 1886. No more appeared by local playwrights, it seems, until the late twentieth century.

That Emerson (1909:92–94) discusses at length only four of the puppet actors and only one play—and that based on oral tradition—may reflect the greater age of these puppets, this play's popularity, the puppeteer's desire to describe his greatest success, and Emerson's wish to support by its traditional content his belief that local puppetry was indigenous. This play, which, of course, could have been composed well into the historic period, was acted by the two sisters, Mailelauli'i and Mailepākaha, and the two rival chiefs, Puapuakea and Makakūikalani. Emerson says nothing of any songs and dances in the play so presumably the originator

Functions and Kinds of Hula Ki'i

used only spoken dialogue and gestures. Nor does Emerson report whether these four images always acted in the same play or sometimes separated to perform in different but suitable roles with other royal puppets.

The playwright's mockery of the four characters is muted and mild. His merry play twits rather than savages them, probably because they are favorite and admired characters. By sharpening distinctive traits and incidents he produced a drama with much suspense that burlesques customs like those of chiefs exchanging challenges, boasts, and insults before a duel to the death, and of aristocratic ladies plotting how to get their men.

The puppeteer is the first and only storyteller known to pair two of the mythical sisters with the legendary chiefs, who, chroniclers state, lived in a pre-European Golden Age when Hawaiian culture had reached its apex. The puppeteer is, in fact, the first to connect any romance with these chiefs. Chroniclers name not a single sweetheart or wife for either although Makakū is said to have had a son. However, the mother's name is not given (Fornander 1880,II;126). The chiefs are famed, not for romance, but for their contests of wit and weaponry. Unfortunately Emerson generalizes about the play without quoting examples of dialogue. The most solemn and matter-of-fact chroniclers, as part of a long saga about King Lonoikamakahiki of Hawai'i, Puapuakea's purported elder brother, did not disdain to quote some of the humorous barbs, often in couplets based on proverbs and riddles, that the two young chiefs or their two "elder brothers" exchanged about them (Fornander 1880,11:114–127;1917,IV:256–363;1919,V:436–451; Kamakau 1961:36,47–63;Kalakaua 1888: 317–331; Beckwith 1940:392–394).

The puppeteer happily revised tradition to allow the young chiefs' "fancies to range abroad at pleasure" (Emerson 1909:93) until the two Mailes captured their hearts and they "settled down to regular married life." Storytellers agree that the two mythical ladies, who like their three sisters move easily from roles in one legend, fiction, or chant to another, are beautiful, fragrant, romantic, clever, energetic, loyal to each other, and faithful to any man or woman they consider worthy of their complete devotion

HULA KI'I: Hawaiian Puppetry

(Beckwith 1919:410ff.;1940:513 *et seq.*). Their best-known role outside orally transmitted art is in S. M. Haleole's mid-nineteenth century novelette written for a Hawaiian-language newspaper (Beckwith 1919). It tells how the five sisters became the devoted attendants of Princess Lā'ieikawai after their brother, the princess's rejected suitor, had abandoned them. It is not surprising that the supernatural sisters are favorites of hula people who sometimes make offerings to them as patrons of dance.

To some chroniclers, the chiefs were evenly matched in every way except physique. Each was the so-called younger brother of the distinguished ruler of his island, his brave and loyal generalissimo, efficient administrator and steward, heir-presumptive, and confidant. But while Puapuakea was short and stocky, Makakūikalani was tall and skinny. A puppeteer can show at least the difference in height by holding Puapuakea lower than Makakū.

Unlike the chroniclers, the playwright sharply contrasts the two in personality. He makes Puapuakea (White Cock's Tail Feathers) symbolize a quiet man of "genuine courage," and Makakūikalani (Royal Boaster) "a rude, strong-handed braggart . . . at heart a bully, if not a coward . . . ever aching for a fight, in which his domineering spirit and rough-and-tumble ways for a time gave him the advantage over abler, but more modest adversaries" (Emerson 1909:92–93). Perhaps other male puppets took part in earlier scenes to demonstrate how he terrorized his opponents. Puapuakea, hearing of Makakū's boasting, challenges and defeats him. The playwright does not follow the chronicles in having Puapuakea kill Makakū; that would have left one Maile sister without a husband and made the play a tragedy unsuitable for a hula of any kind. Instead he has the chiefs compete, not in a duel to the death on the battlefield before their armies, but in a strenuous four-round sports contest in which, after three tied scores, Puapuakea after a hard-fought fourth round wins by a mere three points. In the first three rounds, a different weapon for each round, the puppets first hurl javelins at each other, then throw stones by hand, and next propel stones from a sling. The fourth is a traditional "anything goes" hand-to-hand combat *(lua)* with bone-breaking, eye-gouging, wrestling, boxing, dislocating,

Functions and Kinds of Hula Ki'i

choking, and "tortures and grips unmentionable," as Emerson says. No wonder the two puppets look the worse for wear and one has a broken neck! On the sidelines each Maile sister cheers on her favorite chief as she plots how best to win his heart. The play has a doubly happy ending with both chiefs alive and responsive to the sisters' romantic attentions.

The chroniclers' orally transmitted narratives provided the playwright with a rich source of inspiration. Makakū, certain chroniclers believe, either got bored with the peace and prosperity of the Golden Age or still smarted from insults in his earlier traditional but supposedly friendly slanging match with Puapuakea on Maui. At any rate, he is blamed for getting his renowned "elder brother," King Kamalālāwalu of Maui, to invade Hawai'i, King Lonoikamakahiki's domain. Chroniclers admittedly find no other reason for the invasion. Perhaps the playwright interprets Makakū as especially boastful and combative because of his name and his supposedly having initiated the ill-starred war. Then, too, on the battlefield with the armies drawn up against each other, Makakū, according to custom, started out with the ritual of chanting insults, boasts, and threats at Puapuakea to try to intimidate and terrify him, and boost his own courage. Inexplicably, Puapuakea failed to follow custom by replying in kind! No one has ever explained why; in fact, the playwright seems to have been the first to notice and make good use of this omission in his reinterpretation of the two personalities and their duels of words and weapons from the perspective of an era when native wars had ended.

After this one-sided ritual heard by the assembled armies, the two rivals, again according to custom, fought a weaponry duel. Some chroniclers include a stereotyped incident here (also found in the Kaua'i saga about Chief Kawelo). When Makakū knocked Puapuakea unconscious and thought him dead, his weaponry instructor (a hero always has one with him) advised him to strike the *coup de grace* to make sure Puapuakea was dead, but Makakū, in good Hawaiian hero fashion, scorned this advice as an insult to his mana and martial skill, and angrily replied "A handsome warrior needs no second blow!" Most chroniclers state that

HULA KI'I: Hawaiian Puppetry

Puapuakea revived and killed Makakū, but one narrator (Fornander 1917,IV:348) makes the death comic, thereby showing his opinion of the Maui chief, by claiming that Makakū swung his club from the left so hard that he struck the back of his own neck and died instantly. At any rate, his death was the signal for the armies to take up the fight. The demoralized invaders were routed; even great Kamalālāwalu was slain. However, the death has never diminished the glory of his name or accomplishments —at least not to his many descendants who liken him to "a flash of lightning"(Kamakau 1961:60–61). No doubt the diplomatic playwright had this in mind when he had Kamalālāwalu's kinsman, Makakūikalani, lose to Puapuakea by only three points after four rounds.

Of five other puppets of which he had heard, Emerson tells a little about Nihiaumoe and Ki'iki'i but nothing about Kini Ki'i, Ho'oleheleheki'i, and Ku. Except for Ku, none appears in traditions. Since their names describe status or personality they were most likely typecast in farces about contemporary life, especially in Honolulu where Hawaiians of every rank, king or commoner, were psychologically squeezed between the persistent Hawaiian customs and the conflicting ideal and actual behavioral customs introduced by Westerners. These farces may have been created later than those for the Maile sisters and the two chiefs, just as these four puppets may have been carved before Nihiaumoe and Kini Ki'i who are with them now in the National Museum.

Nihiaumoe's name, which I translate as Midnight Prowler, has a "very suggestive meaning, to walk softly at midnight" (Emerson 1909:94). Nihiaumoe was a bachelor, a libertine, and "an expert in the arts of intrigue and seduction" who sneaked around to women at night. Very likely the constable, Ki'iki'i (Snatcher or Apprehender), would try to arrest him for breaking the new laws against fornication and adultery. Another person presumably under Ki'iki'i's watchful eye would be Ho'oleheleheki'i (Looselipped Image) who, judging from the name, could play the role of either a prostitute (one meaning of *lehelehe* is vaginal labia) or of a male or female informer—a windbag or gabbler. A gabbler is metaphorically and proverbially described as standing like a

Functions and Kinds of Hula Ki'i

loose-lipped image in the garden of Twistmouth *(ku ho'olehelehe ki'i i ka mahina'ai a Nūke'e)* (Pukui and Elbert 1957:183).

Ideally, but not always in actuality, on the side of the law would be Kini Ki'i, who as King Image wears his modern royal purple robe with a majestic air and gives orders to Ki'iki'i whose position in earlier times was that of *ilāmuku,* a marshal and executioner, quick to notice and punish violations of taboos affecting the ruler. Emerson calls Ki'iki'i "a strenuous little fellow, whose duty [was] to carry out with unrelenting vigor the commands of the alii [chiefs], whether they bade him take possession of a taro patch, set fire to a house, or to steal upon a man at dead of night and dash out his brains while he slept." The comment about house-burning: When Chief Kuakini stole Kalanimoku's wife, Kamehameha the Great gave the grieving husband "permission to burn down the houses of chiefs and commoners; that burning was a famous one in history" (Kamakau 1961:389). A puppeteer would never lack for subject matter. Both Policeman and Hangman (with the interesting personal name of Jack Ketch) in Punch and Judy are combined in one stock character in Hawaiian puppetry in Ki'iki'i but no foreign influence was needed to create his character.

No clue occurs to the kind of person the puppet Ku represented. The word *ku* has varied meanings, including "stand," and Kū as a proper name designates a major god as well as numerous historical chiefs and chiefesses, each with one or more distinguishing epithets.

3. Human Participation in Puppetry Acts

Two accounts, one by Emerson, the other by G. M. Damon, describe the different ways in which human beings take part in a show, either in front of or behind the screen, at the same time that puppets perform behind it.

(a) *Entr'actes.* Emerson (1909:93) tells of the custom of having an entr'acte during a performance of a play like that about the Maile sisters and the two chiefs: "Interest in the actual performance of the hula ki'i was stimulated by a resort to byplay and

HULA KI'I: Hawaiian Puppetry

buffoonery. One of the marionettes, for instance, points to someone in the audience, whereupon one of the hoopaa [ho'opa'a, memorizer, that is, drummer-chanter] asks, 'What do you want?' The marionette persists in its pointing. At length the interlocutor, as if divining the marionette's wish, says, 'Ah, you want So-and-so.' At this the marionette nods assent, and the hoopaa asks again, 'Do you wish him to come to you?' The marionette expresses its delight and approval by nods and gestures, to the immense satisfaction of the audience, who join in derisive laughter at the expense of the person held up to ridicule."

Not stated is when these entr'actes occur, but one effective break to build up further suspense would be when the chiefs' contest scores have been tied for the third time. Also an entr'acte intensifies rapport between audience and puppets, who, like live actors, have been playing roles but now seem to unmask in order to communicate directly with spectators and increase the illusion that they are living individuals. Nonetheless, they preserve their mysterious aloofness because, whether they mime or speak with the interlocutor, the screen and staging area separate them from the audience. The human being lured behind or in front of the screen becomes in effect a giant puppet who, like most mythical giants, is awkward, stupid, silly, blundering, and unversed in behaving properly in the strange world in which little people are perfectly at home and can give orders to make fools of big people.

Emerson (p. 97), while giving no example of the ridicule, quotes a *hula ki'i* mele that begins with what seems a dialogue between a puppet and an interlocutor and ends with lines that may have been spoken directly to or about a woman chosen to be teased. The Hawaiian text (with my diacritical marks added) and Emerson's free translation follows. *Kaukau,* a word of several meanings, conjecturally means here "to point out someone in the audience, as the marionettes often did. People were thus sometimes inveigled in behind the screen"(Emerson,p.97,note a).

'Ele'ele kaukau;   Point to a dark one;
Ka halalē, e kaukau,   Point to a dainty piece,

Functions and Kinds of Hula Ki'i

Ka 'e'ele ihi,	A delicate morsel she!
'Ele ihi, 'ele a,	Very choice, very hot!
Ka 'e'ele kūpou;	She that stoops over—
Kūpou.	Aye stoops!
Ka hala, e!	Lo, the hala fruit!

'Ele'ele, 'e'ele, and *'ele* exemplify the way in which a poet modifies a word, which here means "dark." Hala (pandanus) is "a somewhat gross reference to the woman's physical charms" (Emerson). The pandanus tree's globose fruit is a sexual metaphor; the tree's juices and heavily scented male flower are regarded as aphrodisiacs not only in the Hawaiian but other Pacific islands.

(b) *Dancers.* G. M. Damon's account is the only one known to me in which puppets behind a screen and a human being in front of it dance the same hula. But who imitates whom is a puzzle. The occasion for a performance was W. A. Bryan's visit to Moanalua around 1912. Six puppets dressed in red, yellow, pink, and other colors were manipulated behind a white screen by puppeteers, each controlling and speaking for two images. Musicians, number unstated, sat with gourd drums in front of the screen, while standing with them was Namakahelu, Mrs. Damon's principal informant on Moanalua traditional life. When everything was ready, the puppets announced the show's opening by bowing and greeting the audience with "aloha."

Mrs. Damon adds:

> "Namakahelu started the kii chant weaving her arms in and out, now describing a half circle again from right to left, then the hands are brought into her side again. It was a splendid appearance, when one looked upon these marionettes, the drum beaters sat, they face the audience, and back of them was a white cover or screen in front of which were the men and marionettes with their voices."

Probably like many dancers Namakahelu joined in the chant or merely mouthed the words as she danced.

HULA KI'I: Hawaiian Puppetry

It is uncertain whether the only *hula ki'i* mele Damon quotes is the one danced on that occasion. The content seems ideally suited to Pa'akaula's three puppets now in the Bishop Museum— an infant and an adult couple—as does the puppet movement described by Costa (1951:142) of putting arms across the face as if wiping away tears.

The mele, composed like many songs in couplets, opens with a greeting to the sun god, is followed by a couplet about a crying child (*hāpu'u*, "budding," figuratively "child"), and ends with a longer section about a couple making love. Damon does not give the Hawaiian text.

The Hungry Child

Greetings to the Sun there,
Rising from below Kawaihoa.

Hold fast the little child *(hāpu'u)*,
The orphaned child, who weeps.
        Yes.

Little boy, little girl,
The one above, the one below.
Sliding thither,
Sliding hither.
Bubbles burst;
They're washed away by the creek
Into the sacred spring of the heavens.

If Pa'akaula's puppets were performing, probably all three would hail the sun god (Lā), and then one adult would ask the other to take the infant and comfort it. Then they would put the baby away and make love, perhaps with only the drummers chanting.

The trio, as noted earlier, recall Punch, Judy and Baby, and the second couplet adds to this impression except that Mākālei does

Functions and Kinds of Hula Ki'i

not throw Nursling out the window but has Kawehiokanāhele comfort it. However, other Hawaiian meles, borrowing names, phrases, and ideas freely from each other, share elements with parts of this *hula ki'i* chant as well as other types of hula. Emerson (1909:113–114) quotes a dialogue mele for a *hula puili* (bamboo-rattle hula) that has both the greeting to the sun god at Kawaihoa (a point at Ni'ihau Island) and the weeping orphan. The sitting or kneeling performers, each with a split-stick rattle, are in rows facing each other and take turns chanting and making motions. Emerson calls the mele "a fragment of folklore . . . that has drifted down to the present generation and then been put to service in the hula." The goddess Kewelani, it is said, who danced the first known *hula ki'i* to it on Ni'ihau was so comical that the new hula became very popular (Barrere 1980:7–8,63).

> It has come, it has come; lo the Sun!
> How I love the Sun that's on high;
> Below it swims Kawaihoa,
> On the slope inclined from Lehua.
> On Kaua'i met I a pali,
> A beetling cliff that bounds Miloli'i,
> And climbing up Makuaiki,
> Crawling up was Pua, the child,
> An orphan that weeps out its tale.

On the precipitous Nāpali coast of Kaua'i, travellers had either to swim around the precipices in Miloli'i Valley or climb up stick ladders at places like Makuaiki which may make one, according to sayings and poems, feel like a frightened child if one looks up the precipice or down into the valley or the ocean. The weeping orphan and the place names recur in chants by Hi'iaka or Lohi'au when they visited Lohi'au's former mistress on O'ahu and took part in a betting game *(kilu)*. Lohi'au (his love for Pele forgotten) is torn between love for his former sweetheart and for Hi'iaka. As he plays, he chants that he feels as if he were having to swim around Miloli'i because the Makuaiki ladder is missing (Emerson 1915:174). Hi'iaka, in love with Lohi'au and jealous of their hostess but still loyal to Pele, throws the winning toss and tauntingly

HULA KI'I: Hawaiian Puppetry

likens fickle Lohi'au to a child and their hostess to a woman old enough to be his mother (Emerson 1909:179–180):

> Will the orphan now hang his head
> And weep like a motherless child?
> His mother is dead; let him weep!

There is then more than one Hawaiian source besides foreign influence in which to look for what inspired the Moanalua puppet trio and the mele. And, were the parts about the child and the love-making reversed, a popular Hawaiian, in fact, pan-Polynesian narrative pattern becomes evident. A wandering chief who makes love to a girl at a spring leaves her with tokens of rank for the anticipated offspring who will use them in the future to claim privileges of rank (Luomala 1940). Sometimes the child is mistreated or otherwise unhappy. Variants tell of a highborn child hidden with foster parents to protect it from court intrigues and other threats to its life.

Fosterage and adoption were common in real life not only for endangered infants and orphans but as a privilege among friends, often requested before the child's birth. Kamehameha the Great's children, for example, had many guardians *(kahu),* some present at birth to prevent an exchange of infants. One of the *hula ki'i* chants, to be discussed later, refers to fosterage relating to the Kamehameha family. The practice sometimes created a strong sentimental bond between real and adoptive parents and a hold over the real parents in case the foster parents fell into political disfavor. The bond between the adoptive parents and children was also strong. That it was sometimes hard for parents is illustrated by Ke'ōpūolani's sorrow each time she surrendered a child by Kamehameha the Great to an adoptive parent. With conditions changing under Western influence, she was able to keep her last-born, Princess Nāhi'ena'ena, to rear (Kamakau 1961:260).

20. Pa'akaula and his puppets at Bishop Museum. (Bernice P. Bishop Museum photo)

21. Pa'akaula's puppets, close up. (George Bacon photos)

22. Mākālei or "Magical Fish Stick" in profile.

23. Frontal view of Mākālei's T-shaped torso and hinged arms.

24. Clothed Mākālei.

25. Pa'akaula's puppets, dressed.

26. Puppet family performs at Bishop Museum behind a tapa screen. (Bernice P. Bishop Museum photo)

27. "Punch and Judy," by George Cruikshank, 1828. (Böhmer, 1971)

28. "Punch on his travels," by George Cruikshank. (J. P. Collier, 1828)

29. "Mr. Punch." (Collier)

30–31. British Museum head no. "Haw. 76."
(Ben Burt photos)

32. Berlin Museum für Völkerkunde head.
(Dr. Gerd Koch photo)

33. Berlin Museum für Völkerkunde torso. (Dr. Gerd Koch photo)

34. Sketches painted by Sarah Stone. Upper left sketch illustrates British Museum head "Haw. 77." (Force and Force, 1968)

35. Bishop Museum articulated "doll." (Bernice P. Bishop Museum photo)

36. Bishop Museum unarticulated "puppet." (Bernice P. Bishop Museum photo)

37–38. British Museum head no. "Haw. 77."
(Ben Burt photo)

39. Queen Ka'ahumanu by Louis Choris.
(Bernice P. Bishop Museum photo)

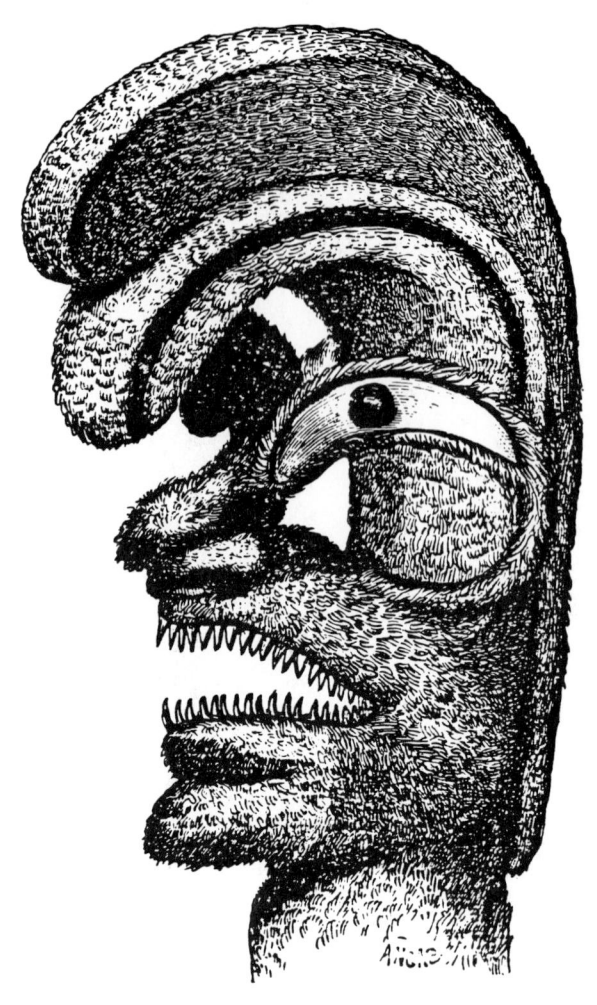

40. "Feather idol." (John Webber, 1778)

D. HULA KI'I WITHOUT A SCREEN

1. **Imitations of Puppets Dancing; No Puppets Present**

A Kaua'i definition of *hula ki'i* as a hula in which "the dancers postured stiffly like images" (Pukui and Elbert 1957:83) may fit the kind Hawaiian and other writers mean when they use the term without explanation. Examples come from Kepelino and Kamakau for the 1780s and 1820s, Kalākaua for 1883, and Emerson for the nineteenth century in general. A second definition of *hula ki'i* as "a dance with marionettes"(Pukui and Elbert 1957:83) is derived from Emerson and sometimes appears as the gloss for the term in translations of earlier Hawaiian-language references.

(a) *The 1780s and 1820s: Kamakau and Kepelino.* The native term *hula ki'i* appeared in print for the first time on February 16, 1867, in one of a series of articles (Kamakau, *Ka Nupepa Kuokoa*; trans. 1961) about Hawaiian culture and history by Samuel Manaiakalani Kamakau (1815–1876). A manuscript mentioning *hula ki'i* was also written around 1867 by Kepelino (Zepherin) Keauokalani (ca. 1830–1878) but not published until 1932 when the Hawaiian text with English translation and other information by Martha W. Beckwith appeared. Each native scholar recorded his own observations in addition to information he had received about the past from highly qualified older Hawaiians. Although both were Christian converts, Kamakau was more objective than Kepelino about customs the missionaries opposed, as is apparent in their references to *hula ki'i,* a term glossed by Kamakau's translators as "the dance with the marionettes," but which from the context of their remarks is "the dance like the puppets."

Kepelino (Beckwith 1932:164–166) singles out *hula ki'i* and three other hulas to name among "the many kinds" danced, and then dismisses all hulas as sinful because "Eyes, hands, feet, and body ensnared the onlooker. The dance taught the young people to sin. He who had known no wrong would quickly learn it in the dance. There was no dance, not a single chant of Hawaii, that was not filthy. But the calling chants and some of the genealogical

HULA KI'I: Hawaiian Puppetry

chants of gods and chiefs contained no double meanings, and the ancestral chants were almost free of them. All the rest of the chants were made by Lucifer."

The four hulas he names may have been those most popular at the time he wrote. Besides *hula ki'i* they are *pa'iumauma* (chest-slapping dance), *kāla'au* (stick dance), and *'ōlapa*. The meaning of the word *'ōlapa* in hula has changed with time, but a simile (Beckwith 1932:132) indicates the type he means when he comments about misalliances affecting chiefly rank that "the chiefs were now up, now down, like the *'ōlapa* dance." He gives no comparable clue to the kind of *hula ki'i* he means but seems to be discussing only hulas by live dancers.

Kamakau, without judgmental comment, describes two noteworthy occasions when the *hula ki'i* and other hulas were performed, but he, no more than Kepelino, tells the kind of *ki'i* dance he means.

In his history of the last years of King Kalani'ōpu'u, Kamehameha the Great's paternal uncle and Cook's friend, who died in 1780 or 1782, Kamakau (1961:105) states that the King, even into his eighties, loved both to hula and to watch hula, with the most popular dances being the *kāla'au*, the *'āla'apapa* (dignified, classical dance), and the *hula ki'i*. Kamakau remarks: "Everyone, young and old, even to the babies just able to walk, was summoned to dance before him. . . . Both chiefs and commoners participated in the dances, Kalani'opu'u, over eighty years old as he was at the time, taking part."

Was Kalani'ōpu'u dancing a *hula ki'i* at the time a young chief criticized his ability? Standing in a crowd of spectators Chief Kapi'ipi'ilani remarked to a commoner nearby, "The hula is amusing enough except for that silly old man's dancing!" Unaware of the critic's rank, the commoner called him a "saucy upstart" for not recognizing the King of Hawai'i. Thereupon his neighbor whispered that he should hush up and not start a brawl, for he was talking to a chief (Kamakau 1961:105).

The mele Kamakau quotes the King as dancing to appears to have a sexual double meaning like many *hula ki'i* songs and the staccato rhythm is also reminiscent. The composer, it will be

Functions and Kinds of Hula Ki'i

noted, has modified *ho'opili* meaning "a narrow or precarious pass" to *holopili* in order to attain three repetitions of the prefix *holo*.

Nu'uanu popo'i ka huna a ka ua.
Kukū ka'ale a ka makani
Hololua, holopili, holokake,
I ke alo o ka pali ka makani.

> Nu'uanu is drenched by the rain.
> Great gusts of wind blow
> Back and forth, against the cliff, in and out,
> Blows the wind at the face of the cliff.

John Papa I'i (1800–1870), without naming the most popular hulas, confirms the King's love of hula in his old age. I'i's family served in Kamehameha the Great's court, and he himself had an illustrious career in the monarchy, starting in boyhood as one of the intimate attendants of Liholiho (later Kamehameha II). I'i (1959:11) remarks about Kalani'ōpu'u:

> Kalaniopuu greatly enjoyed the hula in his old age. When a gathering assembled for the hula and the spectators were waiting to see what kind of dance it would be, he would come forth and stand before the dancers to watch them. With his hands outstretched, he would say to the drummers back of the dancers, 'More excitement! More excitement!' Those who did not recognize Kalaniopuu grumbled, saying, 'The hula is enjoyable except for the interference of that old man.'

Like I'i, Abraham Fornander (1880,II:200) also refers to Kalani'ōpu'u's fondness for hula without naming favorite types.

Kamakau next mentions *hula ki'i* in connection with a great reception in 1821 for the arrival in Honolulu of Kamehameha II from Kailua, Hawai'i (*Ka Nupepa Kuokoa,* Jan. 25,1868;1961: 250). Included was a hula marathon, for dancing was part of

HULA KI'I: Hawaiian Puppetry

every special occasion, joyful or sorrowful. Liholiho loved dancing as much as had his paternal granduncle, Kalani'ōpu'u. An accomplished musician and composer like most Hawaiian royalty, he would drum and chant all night with several equally talented chiefs and, at times, invite other instrumentalists and dancers to participate, after which he gave them presents (I'i 1959:137).

To practice their program for the reception, Honolulu chiefs and commoners—men, women, and children—spent hours day after day. The scope of the program and number of participants may be judged from a single *kāla'au* dance, directed by Chiefess Keana, having "several hundred" dancers. Among the "innumerable" kinds of hulas practiced, Kamakau names seven of which *hula ki'i* is one, and most likely was performed by live dancers.

The Reverend Hiram Bingham (1847:123–125) was displeased by the noisy practice and heathenish behavior that went on for "several weeks in succession" near the Governor's house. Early every morning drum beats called the populace of every rank to collect loads of rushes which they carried on their backs to spread as a carpet on the outdoor dance ground. Then, performers, naked except for dance ornaments, began their arduous practice of dances, songs, and instrumental accompaniments. Bingham comments, "The whole arrangement and process of their old hulas were designed to promote lasciviousness." It also promoted "idolatry," for the dancers cast their used wreaths at a nearby hula shrine as offerings to the hula gods.

Once he protested to Liholiho and Kamāmalu, one of the King's five queens, about the dancing, games, and other old customs performed on the Sabbath and during a period of mourning. To him it was the continuance of worship of the "foolish gods" of old. The royal couple replied that hula was "*play* not idol worship" (p. 129). Throughout Liholiho's brief reign (1819–1824), hula was taught and danced throughout the kingdom.

Kamakau's reference to *hula ki'i* for the 1780s raises the question of whether he projected it from his own era into Kalani'ōpu'u's. The reference for 1821, however, is unquestionable,

Functions and Kinds of Hula Ki'i

for it seems reasonable since puppet dances are confirmed in 1820, that human imitations of their motions were being done.

David Malo (ca. 1793–1853), oldest of the converts writing about their Hawaiian culture, does not list *hula ki'i* among the ten dances he names in his few lines about hula in a manuscript he completed in 1839 (Malo 1951:231). Yet, before his conversion he had been "a master in the arrangement of the hula," according to N. B. Emerson, his translator (Malo 1951:viii). After abandoning the old system, including its amusements, Malo felt obliged, comments Emerson (1909:107–108), "to denounce it root and branch," and consequently probably listed not the ten most important hulas but those first coming to mind.

The social struggle over hula, including *hula ki'i,* that started with the missionaries' opposition, continued through the nineteenth century and well into the twentieth. To critics, certain types (*kāla'au,* stick dance) were attractive calisthenics perhaps, but they found it simpler to eliminate all hula in order to get rid of those appealing to baser instincts. Moreover, it wasted time better spent, for example, in sewing clothes to cover nakedness decently and earning money to buy the cloth. *Hula ki'i* especially suffered because it was particularly intended to arouse laughter by the often suggestively bawdy antics of puppets or human imitators; also the term *ki'i* implied "idol worship."

In spite of attacks on hula, even *hula ki'i* remained a popular dance into the 1850s, as evident from its inclusion in the repertoire of the Hawaiian hula troupe travelling in California during Gold Rush Days. For dancers it had the advantage of letting them catch their breath in the more limited motions and of providing a change of pace and style.

When N. B. Emerson, defender of traditional hula, wrote that "modern hula" was not "a fair and true representative" of the art because of white influence, W. D. Alexander replied that even among the ancients the worst forms were the most popular and have survived, and the whites have helped keep this "relic of heathenism" alive (Malo 1951:231, note 1 by Emerson and Alexander). To Oliver P. Emerson (1928:210) the hula drum that he

HULA KI'I: Hawaiian Puppetry

and Nathaniel had heard so often during their childhood was not "a call to an innocent dance," but "an insidious evil," bringing with it "intoxication and licentiousness in those of weak and loose character."

From 1819 on, hula in which Kalani'ōpu'u had delighted became a symbol of cultural and social alienation from behavioral standards and way of life advocated by the Protestant reformers and their more faithful followers. It was not until after World War II that some organizations permitted members to do any except seated and "calisthenic-type" hulas. Now there is a revival of hula and traditional training as a social protest against the loss of ethnic identity through the cultural assimilation and "Americanization" that was an integral part of nineteenth-century foreign goals in the islands.

(b) *1883, Kalākaua's Coronation.* On February 24, 1883, four *hula ki'i* by human dancers were on the nearly eight-hour-long program of hulas and chants, an official part of King Kalākaua's celebration of his coronation ceremony on February 12, nine years after his accession. To revive ancient hulas, create new ones, and train performers, he had brought hula masters from other islands to Honolulu. For his program written in his own hand in Hawaiian for the printer, he listed the name of each hula master responsible for a sequence of dances and chants and specified the type of hula for each mele for which he gave the title or the first line (the Program is reprinted by Barrère, Pukui, Kelly 1980:133–139). Followers of the "Palace crowd," the King's admirers, held nightly impromptu hula programs throughout the celebration.

The King organized his coronation ceremony and celebration as a "one man show," with "as much finesse as any of the elaborate productions he had observed while a guest of the monarchs of Europe and the Far East. . . ." "He demanded such a variety of ability to perfect his programme, that all available amateur talent in the royal kingdom was enlisted for various parts of the elaborate ceremonials and pageantry. . . ." (Frowe 1937:82). Always interested in theater, the King planned his coronation, which took three years to prepare, as "a legal dramatization. Each scene was

Functions and Kinds of Hula Ki'i

as carefully planned as the acts of the finest plays Kalakaua saw on his trip around the world in 1881" (p. 68).

The Coronation Hula Program was held in front of the newly completed Iolani Palace in a temporary amphitheater seating around 4,000 spectators. Outside were nearly 5,000 trying to see the show. After a luau, the dances began around 4 P.M. and continued until nearly 11:30 P.M.

Ehu Keohohina, one of the seven hula masters on the program, directed a sequence of thirty-two dances. Each of his eight different categories of hula types has four examples; the first lines of the four in the final category, that of *hula ki'i,* are:

1. He poni hanohano nou a Kalani.
2. Eia Wewehi hi-keke.
3. Eleele kaukau.
4. A ka uka au i Halemano-e.

Renditions in Hawaiian and English of Nos. 2 and 3, but not of Nos. 1 and 4, have been published by Emerson (1909:94–97). No. 1, "Your crown is glorious, O heavenly one," was composed for the coronation. Winona Beamer tells me that she saw Mrs. Jenny Wilson dance this praise chant with quick, stiff puppet-like movements. All four dances, I infer, were by human dancers imitating puppets. No. 4, "Oh, the distant upland rising at Halemano," is perhaps romantically lyrical, with metaphors about love inspired by the landscape in this mountainous area on O'ahu, "a region of legend and romance," as in a hula chant attributed to poetic Hi'iaka who, thinking of Chief Lohi'au, sings that "sweet is the thought of . . . our mountain retreat, Halemano, . . . fenced from each other by tabu" (because Lohi'au is her sister Pele's lover) (Emerson 1909:242).

No. 3 on Kalākaua's list of *hula ki'i,* "Ele'ele kaukau" (Point to a dark one), was quoted earlier in Hawaiian and English from Emerson (1909:97).

No. 4, "Here's Wewehi!" (the meaning of *hikeke* (hī-ke-ke?) in the title as given by the King is obscure) is printed in Hawaiian and English by Emerson (1909:94–96), who, learning several renditions, quotes the twenty-one lines of one and four of another to show that variations do "not greatly change its character." The mele is contrarily both an elegy and a satire about Wewehi (translatable as Decorative), who is said to have been a Maui princess and "a flirt-errant, luxurious in life, quickly deserting one lover for the arms of another; yet withal of such humanity and kindness of fascination that, at her death, or absence, all things mourned her. . . ." In his variant, which has the opening line of "E Wewehi, ke, ke! (O Wewehi, la, la!), the metaphor of the couch in the waist of a double canoe refers to Wewehi's body and the canoe paddlers are her lovers. When she dies from "the wound of Maui" (the anus and probably other apertures in the unfinished human body opened by the demigod), "the flag weeps at half-mast," and the number of such "cast-down flags" is "a scandal." The flags probably refer euphemistically to Wewehi's lovers' sexual parts.

As to who the hula master Ehu Keohohina was, his island, and his history, I have found no information. In fact, the attempt to identify and learn more about famous hula masters of the past is only now beginning to interest ethnomusicologists.

The "missionary crowd" ridiculed the coronation, deplored the extravagance and sinfulness of these "notorious festivities," and wrote sarcastically about the King's "purity of mind" (Thurston 1936:48–50). Two newspapers called the dance program "evil." The Hawaiian-language newspaper said it "displayed ancient pagan hulas of the time of deepest darkness. . . . The songs were worthless, the words so shameful they cannot be uttered by good people, the thoughts obscene. It is impossible to tell how evil and polluting were the things done last Friday at the Royal Palace" (*Kuokoa*, March 3,1883;trans. Barrère 1980:52). To the outraged *Gazette* (Feb. 28,1883;Dawes 1968:219) the dancers, with rare exceptions, were vicious, and reminiscent of "that monstrous incarnation of brutishness, the benighted, *phallic* worship, whose leprous visage was so horrid that even the Senate of pagan Rome found it necessary to interdict it as an intolerable nuisance. No 'cleanly wantonness' this, but a deliberate attempt to exalt and glorify that which every pure mind must hold as the type of what is to be kept out of sight, and out of mind as the representa-

Functions and Kinds of Hula Ki'i

tive of all that is animal and gross, the very apotheosis of grossness."

The program to William R. Castle (1840–1935), who had it translated, was an obscene publication, so he brought charges against Robert Grieve, the printer, and William Auld, one of the King's aides. Grieve, claiming not to know Hawaiian and to have merely copied the King's own handwriting, pleaded innocent, but the court did not consider ignorance a defense for printing indecent literature. To discuss certain words, the judge, after clearing the courtroom, heard witnesses describe Hawaiian as an ambiguous language and Hawaiian custom as including honoring parts of the body. For printing songs of "gross and incredible obscenity," the judge fined the defendants, but Grieve appealed to a higher court which ruled in his favor (Dawes 1968:219–220; W. D. Alexander 1896:8–9;Thurston 1936:48). Perhaps this legal suit helped the King decide, three years later not to issue a list of hulas for his Jubilee program, which does not even mention the six puppets and their hula at the Opera House. Alexander (1896: 17) did not fail to remark on the absence "this time" (Jubilee) of a printed program "of the nightly hulahulas" at the Palace.

Two of the coronation *hula ki'i*, "Eia Wewehi hi-keke" and "Eleele kaukau," directed by Ehu Keohohina, may have offended Castle and others, but undoubtedly the strongest objection was to the name songs to Hālala (Extremely Large), the personal name of the King's sexual parts *(ma'i)*. A custom, not yet vanished, is to give a personal name at birth to a highborn or favorite male or female child's genitals and compose a name song for them, a type supposed to be "lively and fun" (Elbert and Mahoe 1970:67). Danced to different types of hula, including *hula ki'i,* and usually phrased in nature symbolism, the song, which becomes the individual's cherished possession, may be updated or new songs composed in later life.

Ehu Keohohina's list has at least two such songs. One which is about Hālala is called "Kō ma'i hō'eu'eu," Your Lively Ma'i. The chant in explicit, non-metaphorical language (text and translation by Elbert and Mahoe 1970:67) was danced to an *'āla'apapa,* a type of hula that, according to Emerson (1909:57), was, at its best,

HULA KI'I: Hawaiian Puppetry

as stately and dignified as a minuet! A curious misprint by the printer who claimed ignorance of the language was to substitute the word *moi (mō'i,* king) for *mai (ma'i)* in the title. Another of Ehu's Hālala chants was danced to a *kāla'au* (stick dance).

Discussion of a few other chants of varied types on the Program has been published with translations and texts by Emerson (1909:1915) and Kaeppler (1976:211–214), but as yet there is no assemblage of texts, translations, and discussion of the King's famous Coronation Hula Program as a totality.

c. *Four Other Nineteenth-century Hula Ki'i.* Emerson, besides giving two of the *ki'i* meles on the coronation program, presents four other *ki'i* meles, but does not hint, except in one case, whether live or wooden dancers, or both, performed them. Three are short enough to have been easily danced by puppets behind a screen.

Two meles, although different in spirit, are lyrical love songs. A seven-line song, in scarcely disguised metaphors, gaily invites a lover to an unnamed forest bower, there "O happy bird, to drink from the pool"(Emerson 1909:99). A nine-line mele, turgid in style and filled with names of places, likens lovers to phallic or cleft-like landscape features which pair and embrace. The setting is the Nāpali coast of Kaua'i, where, as the composer tells it, the Lawakua wind first buffets the steep walls of Kalalau Valley, then veers and blows from Kolokini, a tributary valley. Then three pairs embrace: first, two gigantic Honopū cliffs; next, Waialoha Stream with Ko'amanō (a sacred rock in the sea); and finally, Makua Ridge embraces Kalalau Pali. The Pali's overhanging mouth descends, and when the mountain climber's back swings in he feels like a frightened child whether he looks up or down (pp. 101–102).

Emerson (p. 98) freely translates the third ditty, also of nine lines, as a lively invitation to dance and ignores the possible meaning of the words because "the most learned authorities *(kaka-olelo)* in old Hawaiian lore . . . express themselves as greatly puzzled at the exact meaning of the mele. . . ." A dancer, probably Mrs. Jenny Wilson, who gave him the words, told him that "her part was only that of a mouthpiece to repeat the words and

Functions and Kinds of Hula Ki'i

to make appropriate gestures, *he pono hula wale no,* mere parrot-work. The language, she said, was such 'classic' Hawaiian as to be beyond her understanding."

When I repeated this to Winona Beamer, she laughed at the idea of Mrs. Wilson repeating words she did not understand because as a hula teacher she strictly insisted that her students understand the meles. At any rate, Mrs. Wilson's remarks show that a human dancer did this *hula ki'i* and chanted the words at the same time. That Mrs. Wilson may have been genuinely baffled as to the words in the mele is suggested by my efforts to get it translated, which ended with my asking Samuel H. Elbert's opinion. After discussing several possible meanings of nearly every word, he concluded, "So you see there are all sorts of possible translations." I could then see why Emerson went ahead and, as far as I can determine, composed a new poem that perhaps describes the choreography but neither the literal nor double meaning of the song. That he published the text with few diacritical marks makes more modern attempts at translation difficult. One must allow, too, for singers, with the passage of time, having garbled the composer's obscure, obsolete, or obscene words and elisions.

Emerson's text and translation follow (he omitted translating the fifth and the eighth lines):

E le'e kau-kau, kala le'e;	Now for the dance, dance in accord;
E le'e kau-kau.	Prepare for the dance.
E le'e kau-kau, kala le'e.	Now for the dance, dance in time.
E lepe kau-kau	Up, now, with the flag!
E o-ku ana i kai;	Step out to the right;
E u-au ai aku;	Step out to the left!
E u-au ai aku;	[Step out to the left!]
E u-ai ai aku!	Ha, ha, ha!
E-he-he, e!	

Elbert's comments (August 19, 1980, September 21, 1980) regarding this obscure, nonsense chant indicate the difficulties in translating what may be much garbled words. Considering at first my suggestion that *le'e* perhaps should have been written *le'a* (joy), he translated the revised line *A le'a kaukau, ka lā le'a*, "A happy chant, happy day." He added, however, "*Le'e* as a variant of *le'a* seems rather unlikely. It could be a variant of *lēhei*, 'jump' or of *'o'opu le'e*, a 'goby fish'. *Au* could be *a'u* 'swordfish' but since it is used as a verb I doubt this. *Kala* can be surgeon fish, *ka lā* 'the day' or *kala* 'free'. *Kaukau* as pidgin 'eat' was recorded in about 1790, I seem to recall. So you see there are all sorts of possible translations. I don't see any 'right' or 'left' or 'flag'. The *o-ku* and *u-au* lines could be: Stand by (in) the sea, swimming away. *U-* can be a plural marker for verbs. I might favor the following:

Jump/and/chant, free jump.
Jump/and/chant,
Jump/and/chant, free jump.
Turn/and/chant.
Stand by the sea.
Swim away,
Swim away,
Swim away,
Ha, ha.

"Of an entirely different character," the fourth *hula ki'i*, a twenty-three-line mele, was composed, Emerson (1909:100–101) states, for the Hawaiian marriage ceremony *(ho'āo)* of a high-ranking brother and sister. Hawaiians permitted only siblings or half siblings of exalted rank to marry each other, in fact expected it, and sought to prevent a first marriage by either one with a lower-ranking spouse. Such sibling marriages were taboo among commoners. The concern was to ensure an offspring purely of the lineage, of the highest rank possible, so that succession to the rule of the chiefdom or kingdom would not be challenged.

The term *ho'āo* means perhaps "to stay the night through," for "to remain with a woman until morning, broad daylight, was equivalent to declaring her one's wife" (Malo 1951:265, note 6 by Emerson). Companions, who remained to witness the con-

Functions and Kinds of Hula Ki'i

summation, spent the night feasting, drinking, dancing, playing games, and chanting the couple's praises.

Emerson omits the couple's names, the year of the ceremony, and the kind of *hula ki'i* performed to the chant. Internal evidence in the mele and historical data indicate that it was performed in 1834 for King Kamehameha III (Kauikeaoūli) and his sister, Nāhi'ena'ena, the most sacred couple in the kingdom. The Council of Chiefs expected them to marry as they themselves did. Finally, after ten years of mission opposition, the *ho'āo* ceremony for them took place in July, 1834, and the twenty-year-old King followed custom by having it proclaimed in Honolulu streets. Although some Council members were at the *ho'aō*, the marriage was officially ignored, and a few months later the nineteen-year-old Nāhi'ena'ena married sixteen-year-old Chief William Pitt Leleiohoku (Kalanimoku's son) in a Christian ceremony. When she died in 1836 after bearing a short-lived son, fathered, it was said, by the King, the heartbroken King, ignoring the Council's concern over succession, married a low-ranking chiefess, Kalama, in a Christian ceremony performed by Reverend Bingham. When their children died young, two of his nephews (Alexander Liholiho and Lot Kapuaiwa) followed each other to the throne.

That the names of the joint composers of the *hula ki'i* chant are Kaikio'ewa (misspelled by Emerson as Keikioewa) and Kapihe is evidence that Kauikeaoūli and Nāhi'ena'ena are the sacred siblings honored. The two men, important chiefs, expecting to be present when Queen Ke'ōpūolani, Kamehameha the Great's sacred wife, gave birth, arrived late, however, and found an apparently stillborn son, Kauikeaoūli. The infant had been rejected as dead by the chief who was to have become his guardian. Kapihe, a renowned prophet and high priest, started the child's breathing through prayers and manipulations, and Kaikio'ewa was then appointed the infant's most intimate guardian *(kahu)*. I find nothing more reported about Kapihe's later life. The two men may have composed the chant early in the couple's life in anticipation of their future marriage.

Kaikio'ewa filled the role of guardian most zealously throughout his life, and also served Kauikeaoūli when he became Kamehameha III as Governor of Kaua'i while continuing, as from the time of Kamehameha the Great, as a member of the Council of Chiefs. He also became, as Emerson notes, *kahu* to Prince Moses Kekuaiwa, son of Kīnau, the King's half-sister. But for his untimely death, Moses would also have succeeded to the throne like his brothers Alexander and Lot. Emerson, oddly enough, does not mention the important part that the joint composers of the *hula ki'i* had in Kauikeaoūli's life. That Kaikio'ewa attended the *ho'āo* is uncertain, but it is likely, because during this period he often came to Honolulu to try, with other Council members, to control the King's increasing wildness in cancelling new laws and threatening the stability of the kingdom. Renewed hula dancing was, of course, part of his reaction against the numerous restrictions imposed on the kingdom during his continuing minority. (Kamakau 1961:263–265,334–342;Judd 1966:93,n.86.)

The mele is a *ko'ihonua,* glossed by Emerson as "distinct utterance." This describes the style of chanting which, according to Kamakau (1961:240–241), was chanted "almost on one note," with a vibration, a guttural sound in the throat and a gurgling in the voice box. Every word was clear because the voice had to be strong and held in control. The *ko'ihonua* is a poetically phrased genealogy, studded with classical and cryptic allusions to persons, places, natural elements, and events relating to the couple's royal ancestry. Additionally, these allusions are metaphors for the rise of passion and "the celebration of the mystery and bliss of the wedding night, the *hoāo ana* of a high chief and his high-born *kapu* sister. The murmur of the breeze, the fury of the winds, the heat of the sun, the sacrificial ovens, all are symbols that set forth the emotions, experiences, and mysteries of the night"(Emerson 1909:99). The highborn listeners, being well-educated in genealogies, traditions, and poetic composition, could decipher the allusions.

The opening lines state the occasion and begin the series of allusions to the royal couple's maternal ancestors, sacred kings on Maui (who outranked the paternal line), and their famed paternal ancestors on Hawai'i whose lineages sometimes intertwined with

Functions and Kinds of Hula Ki'i

those on Maui. Kihapū (Kiha's Conch Shell)—a supernatural, tooth-studded nautilus—trumpets that Wanahila, said to be a mythical princess, "bides the whole night through" with King Manu'a of Hilo. King Kiha's trumpet, according to Fornander (1880,II:72), was "preserved as an heirloom in the *Kamehameha* branch of *Kiha's* descendants."

Thus Kiha's name in the *ki'i* mele triggers that of his ambitious namesake and great-grandson on Maui, Kihanui (Great Kiha) of the "far-roaming [or, lustful] eye." His fame or that of his successor (the chant is often obscure) spreads even to the Hawai'i of King Keawe'ena'ena, Blazing Keawe, whose epithet repeats that of Nāhi'ena'ena, Blazing Fires. Only a separate paper would do justice to the covert and overt meaning of this *hula ki'i*, the places and events alluded to, the reasons for their being mentioned, the relationship of the persons named to the couple, and the composers' selection of allusions to parallel the rise of emotion. The mele ends with the lines: "Oh, the shout of the Sun resounds,/ The deep sigh swells in Honua'ula [Red Earth]."

No clue is given by Emerson as to whether one or more human dancers, with or without puppets performed this *hula ki'i*. The appropriate gestures in the dance would surely be as deliberate and exaggerated as the chanter's distinct enunciation and rhythm.

2. Human Imitations of Sacred Images, Present or Absent

On Kaua'i, children and adults, after swimming, danced and chanted a *hula ki'i* in the presence of sacred images on the bank of the Wailua River, but their dance, it seems, was not a religious dance. They did the same dance and chant anywhere even where there were no images.

In 1936 Mrs. Keahi Luahine Sylvester Gomes danced it for the Kaua'i Historical Society. Some twenty years later I saw Iolani Luahine, her grandniece and the most accomplished performer of traditional hula, dance it in Honolulu. Iolani, having forgotten this hula, had relearned it from Mrs. Patience Wiggin Bacon, Mrs. Mary Kawena Pukui's adopted sister.

HULA KI'I: Hawaiian Puppetry

Mrs. Pukui (1980:81–82), who directed Keahi Luahine's program for the Society, writes:

> The dance of the wooden images (kii) was originated by the natives of Kalalau on Kauai and did not spread to any of the other islands. In this dance, musicians were unnecessary. The dancer chanted and by stiff posturing told of the small and large wooden images or idols. Keahi told me that small children on Kauai used to dance this on almost all the beaches after returning from a swim. This hula kii of Kauai must not be confused with Dr. Emerson's hula kii or dance in which puppets were used.
>
> The hula kii of Pokii (a place below Kekaha) told of the row (pae) of wooden images (kii) that stood at Wailua, Kauai, near the mouth of the stream. Keahi believes that they are there yet, covered with earth and sand. This row of images was referred to as the 'Pae kii mahu o Wailua' or the row of sexless images at Wailua. Kaia'kea, a kinsman (kupuna) of Keahi, was the last keeper of these kiis.

The accompanying mele with the original orthography and Mrs. Pukui's translation follows:

Pokii ke kii	The Pokii dance of the images,
Hookiikii ke kii,	The images that tilt,
Hoonaanaa ke kii,	The images with protruding abdomens,
Hooualehe ke kii,	The images with knees spread out and bent,
Kaunalewa ke kii,	The images that sway,
Hi'uwai i Wailua,	Washed by the water of Wailua,
Ka pae kiimahu.	Is this row of sexless images
Ua ike a.	They are well known.

When I saw Iolani Luahine do this *hula ki'i* she was in a kneeling position and the only accompaniment was her own chanting of this mele. In writing about the preservation of old Hawaiian

Functions and Kinds of Hula Ki'i

dances by Iolani Luahine and Mary Kawena Pukui, Gurre Pioner Noble, who (1946:40) describes a private hula performance in which Iolani performed this dance, comments: "We were charmed by the unique and amusing chant and hula, The Dance of the Graven Images, of which only a small fragment remains." Fortunately she had Iolani illustrate one pose for a photograph. One wishes, of course, that preservation had begun before the rest of the dance and chant had been forgotten!

From the song one learns that the Pōki'i images, like many full-figured, humanoid, wooden images existing in museums, had their legs separated, knees bent, and abdomens protruding. Their guardian's offerings ensured their good will and maintained their supernatural power which waned if neglected. Whom did the Pōki'i images represent? In the Society's hula program they represented the paddlers of the canoe bringing the Pele family from distant Kahiki to the Hawaiian Islands to find a new home. This special identification is part of the inner meaning of the program for the Society, for "in old Kauai [programs] were never hit or miss affairs without care for order and sequence. One part linked into another, whether the dances were of the same type or not" (Pukui 1980:79). Among Hawaiians, Kaua'i has always had the reputation of being the most aristocratic, blue-blooded, and cultured island in the archipelago.

The program had eight different kinds of hula, set in a framework of preliminary and concluding chants, to develop the central theme, that of Pele's arrival on Kaua'i. A prelude looks ahead to the time when Pele, having chosen Hawai'i as her permanent home, sends Hi'iaka back to Kaua'i to escort her lover, Lohi'au, to Hawai'i. In the program's prelude, the chant is Hi'iaka's call to her sister Kapo, whom she wishes to visit on Maui while on her way to Kaua'i. Then, in the first dance, performed around a fire, Pele's symbol, the chant tells of Pele reaching Kaua'i; the second, a paddling song, is preceded by a prayer that the dancers on the program used as a marching song; the third, the *hula ki'i*, "conveys the idea that the spirits represented by the images shall man Pele's canoe." In the dog hula that comes next, the dog god welcomes the goddess; in the hog hula, also imitative of animal movements, a feast is readied; the stick dance, coming next, symbolizes construction of a shelter; then, after a prayer, a *hula pahu* (drum hula) entertains Pele, and the eighth dance, a dialogue hula, further honors her. The program for the Society ended with several name-chant hulas (not of the *maʻi* type) to honor individuals from the time of King Kaumualiʻi to the present.

Kauaʻi has many places associated with Pele's family. In the neighborhood of the images is Pōkiʻi Ridge, formerly called Pōkiʻikauna (Chanting to a *pokiʻi,* a favorite younger sibling). It is named for Kapo's chanting to her beloved younger relative Moehāuna (Lie Struck) whom she left there (Pukui, Elbert, Mookini 1974:188). The sibling's name suggests that the ridge is her transformed body.

Did the *hula kiʻi* by human dancers originate on Kauaʻi and remain there? Perhaps since the Pōkiʻi hula is the Luahine family's personal property, tabooed to outsiders without permission, only this specific *hula kiʻi* is meant. After all, *hula kiʻi* by human dancers was danced in California in the 1850s, and at Kalākaua's coronation celebration, and most likely was the kind of *hula kiʻi* referred to by Kamakau for both Hawaiʻi and Oʻahu in the late eighteenth and early nineteenth centuries.

More than one island may have created a *hula kiʻi* in which human dancers imitate images as the result of different stimuli, such as the strange images with upraised arms at ʻAhuʻena Heiau on Hawaiʻi; King Kaumualiʻi's puppet troupe on Kauaʻi; and King Kamehameha the Third's puppets most often associated with Oʻahu. There are also a dozen or so narratives and chants, to be discussed in Part III, that have come from Kauaʻi, Oʻahu, and Hawaiʻi and concern magical and legendary images, some sacred, some secular, some activated, and some stationary. Unfortunately the only real-life dance known that imitates images is from Kauaʻi, where, perhaps in the nineteenth century, it originated. Most likely the movements of children imitating the swaying Pōkiʻi images gradually acquired a set form and mele which became the Luahine family's property as the result of one of their elders being the caretaker of these sacred images.

Functions and Kinds of Hula Ki'i

3. Puppets as Human Dancers' Body Masks

In his fictionalized biography of Kalākaua, E. Burns (1952: 113,143) writes of the concluding hula in the program of entertainment in 1863 on the wedding night of David Kalākaua, a High Chief, and Kapi'olani, a High Chiefess, Kaumuali'i's granddaughter:

> Last there came a rarely done ki'ik [sic] hula, a marionette dance, which recited the history of the bridegroom's private parts with the aid of a puppet two-thirds life size. From the naming of the ma'i, Halala, through the ceremony of circumcision, the first intercourse with Tutu, the conquests and a final paean to the bliss of this, the wedding night.

Assuming that the undocumented account reflected an aspect of native puppetry, I considered how the puppet was used. A clue came from the narrative in which a supernatural chief who wanted a sea goddess as his wife hid behind a female image he had made. With his body masked by her image, he gave it a lifelike quality by reaching his arms up to comb her hair. Convinced that she was seeing a sister goddess, the curious nymph came ashore, was captured, and for a time lived with the chief, who later escaped from her by substituting an image of himself when she tried to drown him (Malo 1951:note 17, pp. 86–87; Dickey 1917:35–36). Could the dancer for the newly married couple have used a puppet as a body mask? I found no record of such use.

However, in 1979, Winona Beamer described to me how her grandmother, Helen Desha Beamer, had taught her and her sister as children to use a large, voluminously gowned puppet as a body mask. With a puppet strapped to the front of her body and forehead, each girl crouched down with only her feet and hands visible. In this very fatiguing position each pretended to be a dancing puppet while her grandmother drummed and chanted.

Helen Beamer had learned this hula ki'i from her mother, Isabella Kaili Desha (1864–1949), who had been trained in tradi-

HULA KI'I: Hawaiian Puppetry

tional hula schools on Maui and O'ahu, which were secretly conducted because of legal and social taboos against hula and its teaching. Winona, as a child, remembers that her great-grandmother had a large puppet with "a face like a taboo stick. She'd take a swig of gin, and then she'd squat behind the hula ki'i and chant in Hawaiian and giggle. A lot of the stories were risque. People say it is like 'Punch and Judy,' but I think it harks back earlier than that. The chants we were taught [for hula ki'i] were ancient" (Bowman 1978). In July, 1978, for the Moanalua Prince Lot Hula Festival, two women dancers, each masked by a puppet made by Joanne Beamer, crouched, swayed, and moved hands and feet like a dancing puppet to the accompaniment of a chanter and drummer.

4. Puppet Actors with Human Dancers

Burns (1952:121–123) describes a second occasion, eleven years later, of a puppet used to illustrate Kalākaua's *mele ma'i*. However, the purpose this time was not to flatter and amuse him, but to humiliate him publicly as part of his opponents' political maneuvers to defeat his first attempt to be elected king.

Because Kamehameha V (Lot Kapuaiwa) had died in 1873 without leaving an heir or naming a successor, the Legislature was to confirm a popular vote on two eligible high chiefs, David Kalākaua, and William C. Lunalilo, the late King's cousin. To defeat Kalākaua his opponents seized on gossip to portray him as other than of the "pure Hawaiian blood" that he and his mother and their defenders stoutly maintained.

Kalākaua's enemies not only ridiculed what they regarded as his social and racial pretensions but obscenely belittled his manhood by having, three days before the election, a hula troupe parade Honolulu streets following a carriage driven by a Negro whom gossips proclaimed as Kalākaua's half-brother. In the carriage was a large stuffed manikin—loincloth-clad, black-faced, frizzy-haired, wide-lipped—and labelled "John Kalakaua Blossom." The pretended electioneers following the carriage with the dancers urged everyone to vote for him. Whenever the effigy

Functions and Kinds of Hula Ki'i

was raised to acknowledge bystanders' laughter and applause, a broomstick thrust the loincloth straight out in front. In this insulting setting, the troupe danced undescribed types of hula to Kalākaua's well-known *mele ma'i*. In the short time before the election, Kalākaua, ignoring the wounding personal insults, tried to orate on serious issues facing the kingdom, but listeners jeered and laughed, especially when opponents stealthily put the manikin behind him on the platform. Kalākaua lost the election.

After King Lunalilo's death a year later, Kalākaua defeated Dowager Queen Emma, widow of Kamehameha IV (Alexander Liholiho), for the throne. "The Queenites," verbally and physically, rioted but did not resort to puppetry again to humiliate the newly elected king. However, they and others against him long continued to belittle his ancestry and his claim to being "pure Hawaiian" (Korn 1976:97,227;Field 1937:157,165–166;Thurston 1936:143).

The notion of using a black-faced manikin may have come from the great popularity of black-faced minstrelsy and variety shows (like Fred Millis' for example) with black-faced wooden manikins in their troupes that toured the islands, most often in the last quarter of the century (Frowe 1937). However, these troupes were already coming "in profusion" by mid-century. One company, which arrived in 1849 in Honolulu on a sailing ship enroute from Boston to San Francisco, played a two-week engagement (H.L.S. 1881:36). Not only professional troupes but ships' crews and local amateurs enthusiastically adopted this peculiarly native American theatrical art that combined American Negro and American White cultural elements. Both Caucasians and Negroes cork-blackened their faces to play their roles. It originated in the late 1820s as a one-man song-and-dance act by a black-faced impersonator, Thomas D. Rice, who became popular on both sides of the Atlantic (influencing even Punch and Judy). This minstrelsy after 1842 began to acquire its familiar format with several stock characters and a set format of song, dance, and dialogue. For over four decades, minstrelsy enthralled spectators, but by the end of the nineteenth century it had declined in freshness and popularity (Hutton 1891:89–144; Hornblow 1919,II:107–

HULA KI'I: Hawaiian Puppetry

109). Minstrelsy was only one of many forms of imported theatrical art reaching and influencing island residents from the late eighteenth century on. *Hula ki'i,* it seems, was one of the native forms of entertainment that was adapted to the changing culture of the islands.

PART III
NARRATIVES ABOUT MAGICAL AND LEGENDARY IMAGES IMITATING PEOPLE

A. INTRODUCTION

Hawaiians tell numerous narratives about legendary or mythical men and women who used one or more human-like *ki'i* as a lure, a ruse, a bribe, or a test of recognition (Luomala Ms.) No information even hints that puppeteers ever used any of these narratives in a *hula ki'i* either for a play or a dance despite the suitability of some episodes. Moreover, these movable images apparently were not manipulated like hand puppets but were arranged in an immobile but realistic posture, or made to appear active although stationary, or were magically activated by a god's or a semidivine person's magical power. Nonetheless, the popularity of these orally transmitted narratives, often of great length, about eleven heroes and two heroines who used puppets may have contributed to the notion of making hand puppets.

Most of the puppets that storytellers bother to describe are made of wood; one is of stone. All but two or three are masculine figures. A narrator, to emphasize the image's human appearance, usually describes it from the carver's point of view. It has, he may say, pearl-shell eyes, human hair, ochre and charcoal coloring, and perhaps arms free of the body. Occasionally he gives an image a personal name, but these images are usually called *ki'i ho'opunipuni,* deceptive images.

Four narratives come from Kaua'i, six from Hawai'i, and three from O'ahu. Each may have more than one variant. In one plot, a boy's dancing *ki'i* helps him win a hula contest. In four narratives, men use images to capture women they want to marry, and in three others, images either fight as warriors or act as night guards. Fishermen use images to fool cannibalistic but stupid ghosts, and a goddess escapes from her importunate hostess by substituting images for herself and her companions. Two heroes put images in their canoes as part of their plan either to steal the secret of making fire or to obtain new food plants.

B. THE HEROES AND HEROINES OF THE NARRATIVES

The first narrative to be discussed is from Hawai'i.

1. Kaipalaoa

A little boy named Kaipalaoa, Sea Whale, entered a contest of wits, skills, and knowledge *(ho'opa'apa'a)* against a Kaua'i chief, and bet his life on winning although it was his first contest. The Kaua'i chief was so expert that from the losers he had nearly completed a fence of human bones around his house; Kaipalaoa's father's bones were in the fence (Fornander 1917,IV:574–595).

Kaipalaoa had a calabash of essential supplies in miniature which expanded in size when taken out. Early in the contest he took out his hollow wooden pig *(pua'akukui)*. (Such pigs, it will be recalled, were offered to the god Lono in ceremonies.) The first test was to see whether Kaipalaoa or the chief would be the first to drink kava after first having prepared an earth oven, strangled a pig, and baked it ready to eat. Kaipalaoa wound a cord around his wooden pig to make a squealing sound as if he were strangling a live pig. "What a squeaking pig I have!" he exclaimed. Later, taking it from his earth oven, he extracted from its hollow body his previously prepared package of pork which he ate, and then drank his kava. The Kaua'i chief had to concede defeat in that test.

Next the contestants were to compose and chant hula songs as well as dance. First the chief and his men were to display their skill. The chief's companions were his elderly instructors who helped and prompted him throughout the tests. Kaipalaoa, on the other hand, had no one to help him. For the hula, the chief's men formed two rows, with all chanting their new compositions while the rear row made hula motions.

The storyteller says (pp.580–581):

> When it came to the boy's turn, he placed a wooden image behind him and began his recital. At this the men said: 'It is indeed strange that you should have a wooden image to

make the motions for you, while we had those who could talk and recite with those who chanted.' The boy replied: 'You are all wrong. All great and noted chanters while reciting verses are always accompanied by those who make the motions in silence; the only voice to be heard is from the one doing the reciting. I believe I have the true process, while in your case you were all reciters.

The chief had to admit the boy was right. His disappointed teachers then proposed word-play, certain that they could defeat a little boy. However, he so cleverly matched their punning and riddling verses in his answering verses (in which he introduced the next word to be played with) that the chief wanted to sue for peace and give the boy a fine feast. His teachers, on the other hand, did not want to give up, but finally they admitted complete defeat. Since the contestants had bet their lives on the outcome, Kaipalaoa killed them, baked them in earth ovens, and stripped their bones from their flesh, just as they had done to his father.

Where did the boy's *ki'i* come from? By what means did he make it dance? What did it look like? The storyteller does not say. Listeners and he probably take for granted that the *ki'i* came from the calabash—an enchanted calabash—that his teachers—his mother and his aunt—had given to him. Since the narrator does not call the hula performance a *hula ki'i* it may be that the image was made to dance by magic. Hawaiians have several stories about *ho'opa'apa'a* contests, but only Kaipalaoa had a hollow wooden pig and a dancing *ki'i* (Beckwith 1922;1940:455–463).

2. Halemano

The O'ahu chief, Halemano, is the most lovesick of four heroes who find *ki'i* helpful in winning the women they love. (Fornander 1919,V:228–265;Beckwith 1940:523–525.) When Halemano died of love for a chiefess he had met only in dreams, his sensible, shape-shifting, and magically gifted sister, Laenihi, restored him to life, and located his dream woman in Hawai'i. She was beautiful Kamalālāwalu, Eight-branched Child, namesake of

Magical and Legendary Images

the great Maui chief. The name signified that the bearer was descended from many different branches of great chiefs and gods. Kama's parents had tabooed her and kept her in seclusion with eight hundred dogs to guard her virginity until they could arrange a suitable marriage with someone of equal or higher rank. Halemano's wise sister told him that the only way he could meet the chiefess was through her favorite little brother, Kumukahi, because "she will deny nothing that her brother requests of her." Capable Laenihi then ordered all the people from Waialua to Wai'anae to carve out innumerable wooden *ki'i* and paint them red with ochre and black with charcoal. Other toys were kites, floaters, surf-riding chickens, and large and small red canoes with red paddles, red cords, and crews of red men. Kumukahi was to receive each toy, except the *ki'i*, as he demanded it. He was to get the *ki'i* only after he had called his sister to come out of her shelter. As he wanted the *ki'i* more than anything else he called out to his sister, and then was told to ask her to turn around so that Laenihi could be certain her back was as perfect as her front and thus suitable to marry handsome Halemano who was perfect in every respect. Kumukahi got the *ki'i*.

Halemano won the chiefess's heart, and despite her parents' disapproval the couple with their retinue set out for O'ahu. When the fleet temporarily beached at Hau'ula, O'ahu, Kumukahi, who was in the party, found an undescribed *ki'i* named Malaekahana that so entranced him he refused to leave. The rest of the party went on to O'ahu, but after a few days, Kamalālāwalu sent messengers to Kumukahi ordering him to join her because he must take back to their parents the many gifts Halemano's people had for them.

No more is told of Kumukahi who so much loved to play with *ki'i*. One would like to learn more about him and what his *ki'i* looked like and how he played with them. Probably the children in the storyteller's audience felt the same. As children were free to hear all of the secular tales regardless of subject matter, storytellers often inserted parts of special interest to them. But in the case of Halemano, the adult listeners are more interested in what is to come about the tempestuous married life of the couple, which takes more than one night to tell. The couple's final and permanent separation and estrangement is predictable, for, as Beckwith (1940:525) comments, Hawaiian "stories which end with a happy married life must be suspected as a foreign innovation."

3. Kauakāhiakawa'ū

Wooing a sea goddess and then living with her created problems not only for Chief Kauakāhiakawa'ū of Kaua'i but for Chief Konikonia of Hawai'i and the god Wākea. Each had recourse to one or more images during their affair. Storytellers have drawn on a shared reservoir of names and incidents about these amorous relationships between land-dwellers and sea-dwellers.

Male and female images enabled Kauakāhiakawa'ū, The Chilly Forest Rain, to first lure a sea goddess ashore, then test her recognition of him, and finally escape when she dragged him into her watery element (Malo 1951:note 17,pp.86–87 by N. B. Emerson). The handsome chief's name tells much about him, for both coldness and rain reappear in Hawaiian love chants and tales to symbolize sex. And the forest, especially on a mountain, is where many of the romantic chiefs and chiefesses live in luxurious seclusion waiting for the spouse of their dreams. In the best-known narrative about him, Kauakāhi woos an earthly, tabooed chiefess with music from his two magical nose flutes rather than with images (Beckwith 1940:526–544;Thrum 1923:123–135). Lovers use nose flutes to breathe their love calls near sleeping women, but Kauakāhi's magical call was heard across a mountain by a sheltered young girl who ran way from home and travelled through many dangers to the source of the music. It is relevant to mention that this chiefess was tested by the chief's guardian, an old woman, to see if she knew which man she wanted. The girl rejected the man offered her and went to sleep at Kauakāhi's side.

The chief did not win the sea goddess as easily. He had fallen madly in love with "a beautiful and voluptuous" sea goddess whom he had seen "disporting herself in the ocean," and then coming to shore to climb up on a rock to comb her hair with her

Magical and Legendary Images

fingers. To trick her so that he could catch her, the chief carved a stone image, "a very perfect representation of the human body, even to the hair." The image, which he called 'Onoilele, Tempting Flight, resembled the goddess, who was Ulipo'aiokamoku, Uli Dark Encircler of the Island. Whether she was the namesake or that Uli known for her evil ways is not clear. After seating the image on a rock at the shore, Kauakāhi hid behind it (using it like a body mask), provided it with a voice, and extended his arms forward to comb seaweed out of its hair with his fingers as he had seen Uli do. At first Uli dismissed the puppet as "a sham, an image" but when the chief shifted its position it looked so lifelike that Uli thought it a sister goddess and came to meet her. After making the image disappear (no doubt by magic), Kauakāhi made "hot love" to Uli. Then they went to his feather-covered mountain home in the rain forest where the chief disappeared. However, Uli saw a row of humanoid images and an old woman who asked her to choose her husband from the row. Going from one to another, she finally chose an attractive but heavy image to kiss. It was her husband. (He had either hidden inside an image or transformed himself into one—the storyteller does not explain.)

After some time the couple visited a god, a friend of the chief's, who warned him to always keep his image with him because Uli was dangerous. Sure enough, on their way home, Uli dragged the chief into the Wailua River, apparently intending to pull him out to sea to her home. He nearly drowned before he could substitute his image, be rescued by his pet birds, and escape to land. There his flocks of pet birds lifted him up on their wings and flew the exhausted chief back to his mountain home.

A brief variant of the narrative omits the test by the row of images but retains the female image as a lure and the male image as the chief's means of escape (Dickey 1917:35–36).

Without the Hawaiian-language texts it is difficult to determine how much of the story's Western flavor results from its retelling in English. The setting and the three episodes relating to the images occur in other Hawaiian narratives and are clearly local inventions. Uli, however, resembles Western mermaids who live increasingly unhappy and discontented lives ashore with land-based husbands. Uli, like them, sits as a siren on a rock near shore to comb her hair and tempt human men, but unlike them she combs her hair with her fingers, not with a golden comb. Neither does she sing magical songs—music is Kauakāhi's special art—to lure a man to a watery grave and thus get the soul she lacks. Uli does indeed try to drag the chief to a watery grave but nothing is said of her intent to thereby take his soul for herself. None of the Western stories, so far as I know, use images in connection with the mermaids as Kauakāhi does. He is more the aggressor than the apparently reluctant Uli, and no mermaid has been taken to such an unlikely home as that in a mountain forest. In this unhappy romance, Uli deserves sympathy. The narrative is probably a nineteenth-century Hawaiian storyteller's spinoff from the better-known plot about the chief and his magic flutes to which elements of Western mermaid lore have been added.

4. Konikonia

Chief Konikonia of Hawai'i captured a sea goddess, Wahineimehani, Hot (or Unapproachable) Woman, as his wife with the help of her brother, Kū'ula, Red Kū, who told him she was inordinately fond of images and had even married one (Malo 1951:234–237;Fornander 1919,VI:318,from Malo). Because the Hawai'i chief had befriended Red Kū, who had been exiled from his undersea land, he told him not only that it was his sister who had been breaking fishermen's lines and taking their bait but that he knew how to trick her ashore so that Konikonia, who was fascinated by hearing about her, could marry her.

Red Kū explained that his sister's husband, Ki'imaluahaku, a *kāne ki'i,* male image, was away just then. What Konikonia must do is deceive her with an image at her door which she would mistake for her returned husband. Then a succession of images tied to a line, each a fathom apart, would lure her to the surface. Images standing on shore would draw her on until they led her into Konikonia's house where a recumbent image would lure her to lie down beside it and sleep.

Magical and Legendary Images

The brother's advice on how to make this last image probably applies to all: "Just carve a large image; smooth it off nicely and paint it of a dark color; let it have eyes of pearl; cover its head with hair; and, finally dress it in a *malo*" (Malo 1951:235).

The plan worked. Wahineimehani went from one image to another, kissing it, until she reached the last and lay down to sleep beside it. There Konikonia found her.

When she asked for her "usual" food, the chief sent a diver to fetch it from her homeland. When she opened the calabash a crescent moon flew out and into the sky. Later she warned her husband that her parents would send her fish brothers in a tidal wave to engulf the land and take her home. The couple and their people then fled to a mountain top from which the highest wave receded as it touched their door, and they were saved.

Another version entirely omits the section about the images (Fornander 1919,V:266–269), but clarifies some points. Her brother (here called Kīpapalauulu, Breadfruit-Leaf Pavement) asks her (here called Hina'aimalama, Hina Eating the Moon) to leave their undersea home and marry his friend, Chief Konikonia. He tells her that it was because of her that he had been exiled—their parents had driven him away because he had once failed to guard her, their favorite and tabooed child. Before going into exile he had, however, given her a calabash of moon and stars to eat, her usual food.

Hina and Kīpapa were the most human looking of their mother Coral-vomiting Hina's ten children. The others, all shape-shifters, could take such forms as fish, roosters, or hens. One undescribed daughter's name is Ki'imalu(a)haku, the same as Wahineimehani's first husband's name. Konikonia and Hina also have ten children, all of whom could transform themselves into forms of marine life. This version has neither the bride's request for her usual food nor the deluge sent by her angry parents.

Although the name Ki'imaluahaku could be translated Ki'i of the Sea Breezes, the descriptive epithet *luahaku* is more likely a cognate of Ruahatu, the name of a Tahitian and Marquesan character, as Emerson points out (Malo 1951:237, note 3). In central

HULA KI'I: Hawaiian Puppetry

Polynesia, Ruahatu, Abyss Lord, is a sea god, who, in Ra'iatean myths, floods the land after two fishermen's hooks catch in his long hair as he sleeps in his ocean cave. The name is also a flattering epithet for Tinirau, a pan-Polynesian sea god who fascinates young girls and lives on a floating island with mirror pools in which he admires his looks (Luomala 1955). Young girls, scolded at home for misbehavior, run away to live with him, which they usually regret later. Fish are Tinirau's subjects, and two of them, either sharks or whales, are his pets who provide him with transportation.

The two versions of the narrative about Konikonia and his undersea moon goddess supplement each other in ways that suggest a longer and more complete version may have existed, and that later storytellers have retold what they remembered, and added new material that they share with other Polynesian narrators. Coral-vomiting Hina and Moon-eating Hina are well known from their experiences with the god Wākea, who also was entranced by sea goddesses.

5. Wākea

Wākea, Atmosphere, is like Konikonia in having a wife who is goddess of both the sea and the moon, and like Kauakāhi in testing her ability to recognize him in a row of images. These motifs appear in a few cryptic, obscure, and symbolic lines in the 2000-line sacred creation chant, Kumulipo, Origins in the Deepest Darkness (Beckwith 1940:217ff.;1951:117–127). The property of King Kalākaua and his sister, Queen Lili'uokalani, it traces the family's divine origin and history to the beginning of the world. For the Wākea motifs, it provides a minimum date of approximately 1700 A.D. because the Queen estimated that at that time the poet Keaulumoku had arranged the chant in its present form. However, the wide Polynesian distribution of many of the motifs leaves no doubt that their Hawaiian expression is far older than 1700 A.D. It is likely that the stories about Konikonia and Kauakāhi have taken bits from the chant about Wākea.

Wākea, finding a canoe bailer *(ke kā)* floating in the ocean, put

Magical and Legendary Images

it into his canoe where it became a beautiful woman named Hina Kekā (lines 1903–1908). She was really Hinaikamalama, Hina the Moon (her sobriquets vary) who ate the "seeds" (stars) strewn in the heavens. After taking her home, Wākea set her beside the fire, a euphemism for the sex act, and, like Coral-vomiting Hina, she bore corals, eels, sea urchins, and volcanic stones, and changed her name to Hina of the Coral-producing Womb (lines 1909–1913).

The enigmatic next line "Hina craved food, Wākea went to fetch it" is understandable from her being Hina of the Moon like Konikonia's wife and wanting her usual food. However, the double meaning has to do with sex. That the moon goddess is also the sea goddess is no surprise in view of the moon's effect on tides.

The next lines (1914–1918) introduce another familiar motif:

[He] set up images on the platform,
Set them neatly in a row.
Wākea as Ki'i slept with Hina the Reddened One.
Born was the cock, perched on Wākea's back.

The different Hawaiian-language renderings of this passage raise the question whether this Hina is Hina of the sea and moon, or another Hina. The images, as is evident from the narrative about Kauakāhi, are a means to test whether or not Hina can recognize and accept her husband in this new form. Konikonia's wife, it will be recalled, had an image who was a sea god as her husband. The term *ki'i* has complex meanings besides that of image. The Kumulipo calls the first man Ki'i, who with his sister La'ila'i, Calm, and his two brothers, Kāne and Kanaloa, was born at the end of the Night World (Pō), the first cosmic era. In the Day World (Ao), the era of living men, La'ila'i mates with Kāne, a god who is a symbol of procreation and now the term for male. However, La'ila'i causes a scandal when she leaves Kāne to live below in Lua, Pit, with Ki'i, a mortal man. The scandal is that a goddess should have a misalliance with a human being.

In southern Polynesia, the word *ki'i* (cognates *ti'i, tiki*) also means image, and as a proper name refers to the first man and sometimes is the personal name for Kāne's genitals. This double meaning of Ki'i may fit Wākea's cognomen when he mates with Hina the Reddened One. It is also apparently a misalliance in some way because the impudent cock that is born to her and perches on Wākea's sacred back is a metaphor for a chief, especially one of lower rank, seeking to usurp a legitimate chief's place. A little later in the Kumulipo, the cock seems to be the demigod Māui, who strives against superior-ranking gods of land and sea. Wākea is not specifically identified as his father except that Māui's mother is Hina of the Fire, which may be another name for Hina the Reddened One. In variant prose tales, Hina the Bailer is Māui's wife whom he finds floating as a bailer in the ocean, and who helps him tie the islands together. Names and incidents obviously shift freely from one plot to another. Characters like Hina have innumberable sobriquets to become independent beings.

6. Māui

The demigod Māui uses an image of either tapa, wood, or gourd, to deceive goddesses in order to learn their secret of making fire. They reluctantly give him firebrands but carefully hide how they make it. These women, who can assume the form of mudhens, keep a close watch on Māui's whereabouts so that they can keep their secret and not share it with him and the rest of the world. Each day when the Māui brothers go out fishing in their canoe, the mudhens count the number in the canoe to make sure the tricky youngest one is there. However, the dummy he set up in the canoe fooled them. He sneaked up on them, grabbed the youngest mudhen, and forced her to teach him every detail in making fire. Exasperated with her delaying tactics he hit her on the head with a burning stick and made her and other mudhens permanently bald. (Forbes 1879:59–60;frequently reprinted, as by Thrum 1907:33;Fornander 1919,V:560–564; Westervelt 1910:61–65;Pukui and Curtis 1960:32.)

41. Kamehameha The Great
    Dates of reign 1795–1819.
    (Bernice P. Bishop Museum photos)

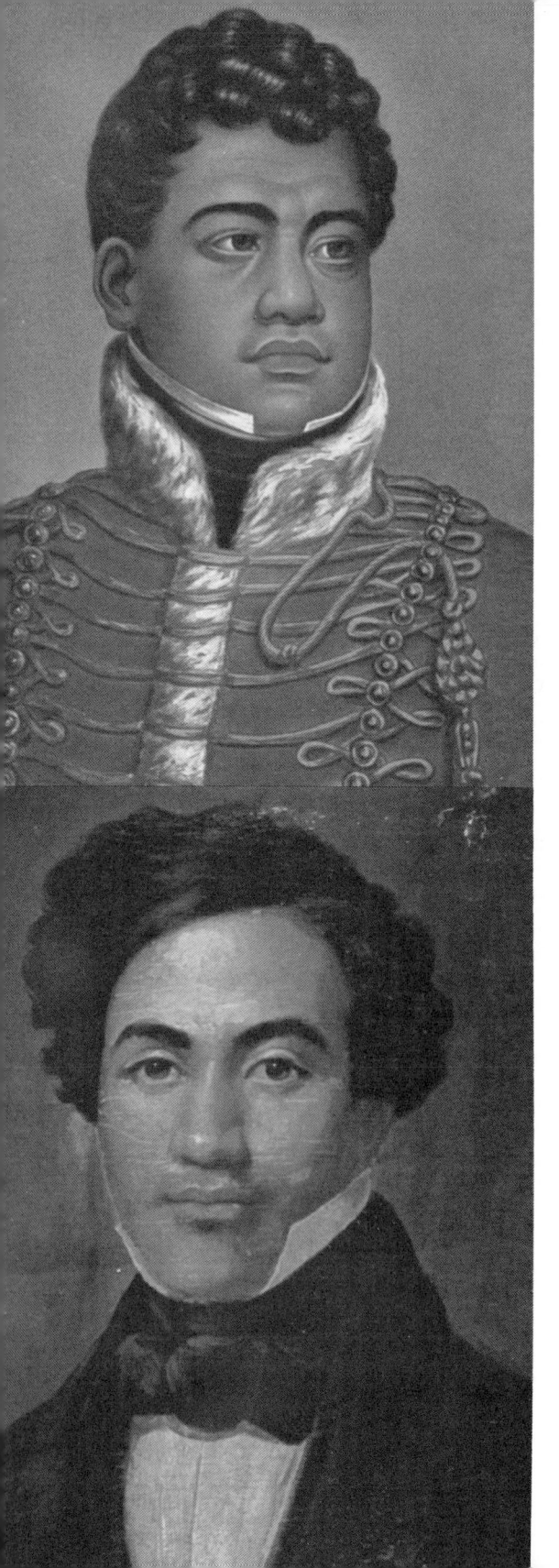

42. Kamehameha II (Liholiho)
    Dates of reign 1819–1824.

43. Kamehameha III (Kauikeaoūli)
    Dates of reign 1825–1854.

44. Portrait of Nāhiʻenaʻena, Sister of Kamehameha III, oil on canvas by Robert Dampier, 1825. (Honolulu Academy of Arts photos)

45. Kamehameha III, companion portrait by Dampier.

46. Kamehameha IV (Alexander Liholiho)
    Dates of reign 1854–1863.
    (Bernice P. Bishop Museum photos)

47. Kamehameha V (Lot)
    Dates of reign 1863–1872 (or 3).

48. William Charles Lunalilo
    Dates of reign 1872 (or 3)–1874.

49. Kalākaua (David Kalākaua)
    Dates of reign 1874–1891.

50. Lili'uokalani (Lydia Paki)
    Dates of reign 1891–1893.

51. King Kalākaua Coronation, 1883.
    (Bernice P. Bishop Museum Photos)

52. Dandy Ioane and Hula Girls.

53. Winona Beamer Hula Troupe performing *hula ki'i* at Moanalua Gardens, Prince Lot Hula Festival, Honolulu, 1978. (Winona Beamer photos)

54. Winona Beamer and dancers perform *hula ki'i*.

55. Modern puppet stage at the festival.

56. Women dancers wearing body masks perform *hula ki'i*.

57. Boy dancers with hand puppets at the festival.

58. Iolani Luahine in *hula kiʻi* pose: The Dance of the Graven Images. (G. P. Noble photo, *Paradise of the Pacific* 58:38, 1946)

59. Mary Pukui and her daughter, Pele. (Martha Homsey photo, *Paradise of the Pacific* 58:39, 1946)

Magical and Legendary Images

7. Pūpūhulu'ana

Another hero who had an image in his canoe was Pūpūhulu'ana, Tuft of Red Feathers, but he had made his of wiliwili (the same wood of which the six National Museum puppets are made). Like Māui he wanted something from divine beings who were relucant to give it. Because his district on Hawai'i was barren and needed food plants, Pūpū sailed off with his *ki'i* to a distant land where he hoped gods would give him some plants. They declared, however, that he could not have them until he had passed a test by answering their many questions correctly. When not a single question stumped him, they concluded that the image in his canoe was that of his guardian god whose spirit had entered it to help him in the test. Actually, the answers came from one of the gods' fishermen who had befriended Tuft of Red Feathers, and lay hidden in the canoe beside the image. (Fornander 1917,IV:570–573;Beckwith 1940:430–432.) An incomplete version states that Tuft of Red Feathers uprooted a large ohia tree *(Eugenia malaccensis)* from which to carve two *ki'i* to resemble the gods' famous humpbacked fishermen. Tuft of Red Feathers gave the images shell eyes, real hair, and "everything complete." There the story ends so how he used the images is unknown. (Thrum 1925:90–95, translated from *Ka Nupepa Kuokoa*, August, 12, 1865.)

8. Kau'ilani

Three narratives tell of soldiers using images as active warriors or passive guards. One of these stories is about Kau'ilani, Heavenly Athlete, of Kaua'i, whose guardian gods gave him an army of wooden warriors magically activated, in order to kill his father's supernatural enemy, a terrible monster (Thrum 1923:171–178; Westervelt 1915:204–205). The wooden soldiers fought bravely although the vicious monster's sharp teeth shredded many to pieces. Finally Kau'ilani and his surviving warriors killed the monster, and he offered its body and the remains of his fallen warriors as burnt sacrifices to his helpful guardian gods.

HULA KI'I: Hawaiian Puppetry

9. Kawelo

Storytellers have added incidents as afterthoughts to the saga of Kawelo of Kaua'i who won the war against usurpers who had seized the island from his royal parents. One such incident tells of Kawelo and his brother finding a way to sleep at night without worrying about a surprise attack. They made images of themselves and seated them by the fire to make the enemy think they were awake and on guard (Dickey 1917:22).

10. Pi'imaiwa'a

One of the greatest fighters and generals of King 'Umi-a-Liloa, Hawai'i, during the sixteenth century was Pi'imaiwa'a, who was renowned throughout the islands for his strength and fearlessness, and added further glory to his name in a battle on Maui. The enemy fought by day on the plain but at night climbed a sixty-foot ladder to the top of Kau'iki Hill, Hana district, where they slept peacefully undisturbed because they had a giant watchman armed with a huge war club standing at the top of the ladder. Two of Great 'Umi's generals, who started to climb the ladder to kill the guard, turned back in fear. Then Pi'imaiwa'a, who had been wondering why he never saw the giant fighting on the plain, climbed the ladder one night. When he got to the top, face to face with the giant, he challenged him to a fight; "He twirled his war club and struck the enemy to the left; twirled it again and struck it on the right. He sent a spear directly toward it, and it moved not at all, but kept standing in one place." Whenever Pi'imaiwa'a struck the giant with his wooden war club there was a thudding sound of wood striking wood. Realizing at last that the giant was only a wooden image, he knocked it over, hence its name Kāwalaki'i, Backward-falling Image. Then the general sent for his men and nearly wiped out all the sleeping enemy. (Kamakau 1961:30; Thrum 1923:84–85; Fornander 1919,V:376–379; 1917,IV:248–254; Beckwith 1940:392.)

A confused account states that after Kamehameha had added the island of Maui to his kingdom he dressed Kāwalaki'i in a feather helmet and cloak and gave him a spear and a war club

Magical and Legendary Images

before dedicating the image to one of his gods (Fornander 1919, VI:692). One wonders if the original image had lasted two hundred years.

11. Kaneopa

Visitors having problems with their hosts resort to images either to get revenge for gross inhospitality or to escape from too much hospitality. Kaneopa, or more correctly Kāne'o'opa, Lame Man, was a member of a Kaua'i party of sightseers led by his chief which was lured ashore on O'ahu by Hanaaumoe, Midnight Worker, at the behest of King Halāli'i. The travellers were promised food, fresh-water baths, women, a canoehouse to sleep in, and many other things. Unfortunately, at this time O'ahu was inhabited only by wicked ghosts. Kaneopa, being suspicious, stayed awake. Every time Midnight Worker came chanting at the door: "Say, say, Halahalakau; say, say, Halahalakau, are you people awake?" Lame Man would then ask when they were to get the food, the women, and all the other things promised to them; they were waiting for them. Midnight Worker always had an excuse for the delay. At last Lame Man dug a hole and hid under the door sill where he knew the ghosts' king would sit. This saved his life because when the ghosts burst into the canoehouse they ate up all the visitors they could find.

Kaneopa managed to get back to Kaua'i to tell what had happened. The high priest recommended that a great many images be hewed out of wood—four hundred, four thousand, forty thousand, 400,000 images *(nui, lau, mano, kini, lehu)*. All the people set sail with the images to O'ahu, arrived at night, and placed some images on the floor of the canoehouse, some under it, and then returned to their canoes to wait for the dawn. The ghosts, seeing them, extended their usual invitation, made the usual promises, and took the visitors to the canoehouse. Midnight Worker visited there frequently to ask if they were awake. But, after a while, they slipped out and hid, waiting for the ghosts to enter the canoehouse. When the ghosts arrived and began to attack their presumed guests, they complained of how tough their victims were. When they saved the choicest portions for their ruler, as was the custom, he too complained of their toughness. Meanwhile the Kaua'i people set fire to the house and burned up all the ghosts (Fornander 1919,V:432–435).

Another Kaua'i storyteller (Rice 1923:68) states that when Kaua'i fishermen slept on the beach at Ni'ihau, ghosts (akua) ate them up. A brave man, determined to make the island safe, built a longhouse, placed inside many wooden, human-like *ki'i* with mottled gray and black opihi-shell eyes, and hid outside. When the ghosts came at night and saw the shining eyes they decided after a time that Kaua'i men slept with their eyes open, and began to eat the images with unfortunate results. "Their teeth were caught in the wood, and while they were struggling to free them, the crafty Kaua'i man quickly shut the door and set fire to the house, and all the cruel *akua* burned to death." Ever since then, this part of the island has been called Ki'i, and fishermen are safe on the island.

12. **Hi'iaka**

It was also on O'ahu that Hi'iaka had to escape unwanted hospitality (Emerson 1915:185). She was on her way back from Kaua'i to Hawai'i with her woman companion and Pele's lover, Lohi'au, whom Pele had sent her to fetch. Their hostess on O'ahu, who was Lohi'au's former mistress, hoped by keeping the visitors longer that she could win Lohi'au from Pele. Hi'iaka was determined to get her party away, for she knew how fickle Lohi'au was. She was famed for her resourcefulness and magical powers, so without her hostess's knowledge she and her party went on their way, leaving behind "unsubstantial forms that had all the semblance of reality."

13. **Hoamakeikekula**

One might have expected that the sea goddess married to Ki'imaluahaku would have had a good chance of bearing children of wood. This did not seem to have occurred, however.

Magical and Legendary Images

Oddly enough, it was Chiefess Hoamakeikekula of Hawai'i, whose name means Companion in Suffering on the Plain, who bore a child that was a *ki'i* and given the name of 'Alelekīnana, Animated Messenger. The father was King Pu'uonale, Hill of Brightness. The birth of their wondrous child marked the climax of a long and often tragic narrative about Hoamakeikekula's life. Born as a taro corm cast away by her parents, she was saved by her grandmother, who, within two days, had transformed it into a beautiful little girl whom she reared in tabooed seclusion. Unfortunately, a bird abducted her to become the lizard king's wife. However, she managed to run away and wandered on the plain without food and shelter, but encouraged by her recurrent dream of a handsome lover to whom her grandmother had promised her in marriage. When Pu'uonale's servant found her and took her to him, the dream lovers recognized each other, and the gods showed their approval of their mating with thunder and lightning, rainbows, floods, red rain, and ten days of mist. The child born to the happy couple was not a real child *(keiki maoli)* but an image child *(keiki ki'i)*. That it was of wood is indicated by Pu'uonale's people getting the idea of making images like it to use in worship. That they put the image child, Animated Messenger, in a heiau as a sacred object is evident from the saying, "Place the image on the sea side of the platform [of the heiau]." (Fornander 1917, IV:532–541;Beckwith 1940:516.) This was one love story that ended happily.

In these narratives, Hawaiians have integrated the concept of human-like images that can be made to simulate the behavior of real people. Except for parts of the narrative about Kauakāhi the accounts appear free of Western influence. The presence of a test by a row of images in the Kumulipo points toward pre-European stereotyping of notions about movable images. Such images are obvious enough to have been invented more than once in Polynesia by a real person in need of a deceptive image or by a storyteller to extend his story (Luomala 1973,1978,1979). With so many notions of images present in reality and in fiction, especially in the Hawaiian Islands, it is likely that the idea of making manipulable puppets for entertainment occurred to someone.

SUMMARY

The ten native Hawaiian puppets now in museums fall into two structural types according to the number of separately made parts in the assembled figures. All examples are small, humanoid, legless images, carved, except for arms, from soft native wood, with the head more realistically carved than the torso. Seven have tapa or imported cloth arm-tubes filled with native vegetal substances; three have arm-slats of imported wood.

One structural type has head, hollow torso, and arm-tubes as separate units. The sole example of an assembled figure has its long neck in a socket in the torso, and cords falling inside after passing through each perforated arm-tube and armhole. Drapery around the base hides the puppeteer's hand manipulating neck and arm-cords inside the torso. Museums also have three wooden heads that perhaps are all that remain of figures of this type. All examples, poorly documented, are in England or Germany. Techniques and materials are like those on wooden sculpture remaining from the half century after Cook's arrival in 1778, but unlike them they establish, among other rarely noted details, that sculptors occasionally assembled figures from parts and pasted tapa directly on the wood. Only one example, a separate head with imported paint on its face, shows foreign influence. This fact, its good condition, and late collection (1881) demonstrate that this structural type continued to be made well into the nineteenth century.

The second and simpler structural type, and perhaps a later one, has head and solid torso as an inseparable unit. Arms (tubes or slats) are on hinges of imported cloth or leather nailed to the shoulders. Gowns hide hinges and the puppeteer's hand moving the arms outside the torso. The nine existing examples in American museums combine local and foreign techniques and materials. However, unlike examples of the first type whose use is unconfirmed, they were actively used in puppetry (*hula ki'i*, image dance), and as time passed hula masters replaced some native materials with those of foreign origin. Information is availa-

HULA KI'I: Hawaiian Puppetry

ble on the names and sex of each example, and something of their roles, types of performance, and history.

Nevertheless, no precise data exist on when any puppet or head was made or when puppetry began. Two trustworthy dates —1783 and 1820—lay a base for conjecture. In 1783, two years before any expedition except Cook's had visited Hawai'i, a sketch was made in England of a separate head. If it was the remnant of an assembled and manipulable figure like the undated, but apparently old, complete example of the first type, Hawaiians had manipulable figures—puppets—by 1778. However, the existence of puppetry was not firmly documented until 1820 when a foreign eyewitness wrote about an entertainment at a royal residence of six undescribed puppets dancing the hula behind a tapa screen to the accompaniment of a drummer-chanter in front of it. What became of these puppets is unknown. In 1816, a foreign artist at a heiau (rebuilt only a few years before) sketched ornamental, unconsecrated humanoid images who had very long, upraised, and perhaps movable, arms. For these references forty years after Cook—as well as later—one must allow for the possibility that foreign contact stimulated hula masters and sculptors to experiment with forms of their indigenous manipulable images and elaborate their patterns of use. After 1820, when Calvinistic missionaries and converts tried to suppress all types of hula, references to *hula ki'i* are rare and obscure until the reign of Kalākaua (1874–1891).

The term *hula ki'i* encompasses varied overlapping forms. Behind a screen, puppets do hulas or even plays, sometimes with a live dancer in front of the screen or a spectator to be heckled. In 1886 the format already established by 1820 was used at the Honolulu Opera House for Kalākaua's guests who saw six puppets, dating from sometime in the long reign of Kamehameha III (1825–1854), do a hula. Perhaps the visits of foreign marionette troupes in 1874, 1884, and 1886 decided the King on displaying publicly the royal Hawaiian puppets. A popular and apparently old form of *hula ki'i,* still done today, has live dancers imitating puppets' dance motions without a screen or puppet present. It may be the form a native scholar, Kamakau, states was done by a

Summary

king and his companions before 1780 and used in 1821 on a program to entertain another king. In Gold Rush days in California, it was done by a travelling troupe; and in 1883, Kalākaua had examples on his coronation hula program. Another form of *hula ki'i* to imitate puppets, probably later in origin, is to have a live dancer wear a large puppet as a body mask. In another form, a live dancer holds or has nearby a large puppet to demonstrate parts of a performance.

Hula ki'i serves only to entertain, mostly as a relaxing interlude or conclusion in a long program; it arouses laughter in spectators of every age by the live or wooden performers' antics and usually ribald songs. Royal patronage continued until the fall of the monarchy late in the nineteenth century. However, hula masters in rural areas maintained the art, added innovations (some perhaps inspired by foreign acts like Punch and Judy), and secretly passed on the art to a few descendants, who further adapted it to continually changing lifeways. Today an occasional hula master keeps alive the tradition of Hawaiian puppetry. With the present revival of Hawaiian interest in their ethnic past, hula masters will doubtless discover more information than I have about earlier *hula ki'i*, and carry on the process of adaptation and invention of manipulable images that existed before 1778, and developed into a form of entertainment sponsored by chiefs and kings and enjoyed by people of every age and class.

That Hawaiians were intrigued by the notion of images acting in human ways is also evident in the several dramatic narratives, often interspersed with chants, that are told on Hawai'i, O'ahu, and Kaua'i. One image was said to have danced the hula and won a dancing contest for a young boy. Other images helped to bribe another young boy who loved to play with *ki'i*, and still others fought bravely on the battlefield or guarded sleeping warriors. Sometimes images acted as substitutes for guests wishing to avoid their hosts. One image married a woman who liked images as lovers, and another took the place of a man who was in danger from his wife. Getting a sea goddess ashore as a prospective bride for a chief or a god was the function of other images, and once ashore the goddess had to choose among several images the one that was her transformed husband. Then there were the images that helped a demigod get fire and cooked food for mankind and enabled a benevolent young man to get food plants from the gods. That a woman could bear a child that was an image, a messenger to inspire people to fashion sacred images, is another notion that occurs in these narratives.

None of these narratives appears to have been influenced by familiarity with either the Kaua'i or O'ahu royal hand puppets. It is more likely that these stories were among the various stimuli which led Hawaiians to make hand puppets for entertainment and to then have live dancers imitate their stilted movements.

BIBLIOGRAPHY

Alexander, William DeWitt. *History of Later Years of the Hawaiian Monarchy and the Revolution of 1893.* Honolulu: Hawaiian Gazette Company, 1896.

Arning, Eduard. *Ethnographische Notizen aus Hawaii, 1883–1886.* Mitt. aus dem Mus. für Völkerkunde in Hamburg (1931) 16.

Barrère, Dorothy B. "Part I. The Hula in Retrospect." In *Hula: Historical Perspectives.* Bishop Museum Pacific Anthropological Records 30: 1–66. Honolulu: Bishop Museum Press, 1980.

Barrère, Dorothy B.; Pukui, Mary Kawena; Kelly, Marion. *Hula: Historical Perspectives.* Bishop Museum Pacific Anthropological Records 30. Honolulu: Bishop Museum Press, 1980.

Barrot, Theodore-Adolphe. "Visit of the French Sloop of War, 'Bonite,' to the Sandwich Islands in 1836," translated from the French. *The Friend* 8 (1850):33–35.

Beamer, Winona, et al. *Nā Hula Hawai'i. The Songs and Dances of the Beamer Family.* Norfolk Island, Australia. Island Heritage, Ltd., 1976.

Beckwith, Martha Warren. *The Hawaiian Romance of Laieikawai (by S. N. Haleole).* Introduction and translation by M. W. Beckwith. Bureau of American Ethnology Annual Report 33:285–666. Washington, D. C., 1919.

_____. "Hawaiian Riddling." *American Anthropologist* (1922) 24: 311–331.

_____. *Kepelino's Traditions of Hawaii.* Bernice P. Bishop Museum Bulletin 95. Honolulu: The Museum, 1932.

_____. *Hawaiian Mythology.* New Haven: Yale University Press, 1940. Reprinted 1970, University of Hawaii Press, with new introduction by Katharine Luomala.

_____. *The Kumulipo. A Hawaiian Creation Chant.* Chicago: University of Chicago Press, 1951. Reprinted 1972, University of Hawaii Press, with a new foreword by Katharine Luomala.

Bingham, Hiram. *A Residence of Twenty-One Years in the Sandwich Islands.* Hartford, Conn.: Huntington, 1847.

Bloxam, Andrew. *Diary of Andrew Bloxam, Naturalist of the "Blonde" on her Trip to the Hawaiian Islands, 1824–25.* Bernice P. Bishop Museum Special Publication 10. Honolulu: The Museum, 1925.

Bloxam, Matthew Holbeche ("M.H.B."). "Curiosities from the Sandwich Islands." *The Mirror* 8 (217), 7 October 1926, Rugby, England.

Bloxam, Richard Rowland. "Visit of H.M.S. Blonde to Hawaii in 1825, as Described by Rev. R. Bloxam, Chaplain, in a Letter to his Uncle." *The Hawaiian Almanac and Annual for 1924* 50 (1923):66–82.

HULA KI'I: Hawaiian Puppetry

Böhmer, Günter. *The Wonderful World of Puppets.* Translated by Gerald Morice. Boston: Plays, Inc., 1971.

Bowman, Pierre. " 'Punch and Judy'—Hawaiian Style." *Honolulu Star-Bulletin,* 21 July 1978, C-3.

Brigham, William T. *Report of a Journey round the World Undertaken to Examine Various Ethnological Collections, 1896.* Bernice P. Bishop Museum Occasional Papers 1 (1). Honolulu, 1898.

_____. *Report of a Journey around the World to Study Matters Relating to Museums: 1912.* Bernice P. Bishop Museum Occasional Papers 5 (5). Honolulu: Bishop Museum Press, 1913.

British Museum. *Handbook to the Ethnographical Collections.* New ed. Oxford: The University Press, 1925.

Buck, Peter H. (Te Rangi Hiroa). *Explorers of the Pacific. European and American Discoveries in Polynesia.* Bernice P. Bishop Museum Special Publication 43. Honolulu: Honolulu Star-Bulletin, 1953.

_____. *Arts and Crafts of Hawaii.* Bernice P. Bishop Museum Special Publication 45. Honolulu: Bishop Museum Press, 1957.

Burns, Eugene. *The Last King of Paradise. A Biography.* New York: Pellegrini & Cudahy, 1952.

[Byron, George Anson.] *Voyage of the H.M.S. Blonde to the Sandwich Islands, in the Years 1824–1825.* [Edited by Maria Graham.] London: John Murray, 1826.

Campbell, Archibald. *A Voyage Round the World from 1806 to 1812.* 3rd Am. ed. Charleston, S.C.: Duke & Browne, 1822.

Charlot, Jean. "Art." *Honolulu Star-Bulletin,* 27 September 1967, B-1.

Choris, Louis. *Voyage pittoresque autour du monde, avec des portraits de sauvages.* Paris: Didot, 1822.

Collier, John Payne. *Punch and Judy.* Edited by John Payne Collier from the performance of Piccini with illustrations by George Cruikshank. London: Septimus Prowett, 1828.

Costa, Mazeppa King. "Dance in the Society and Hawaiian Islands as Described by the Early Writers, 1767–1842." Master of Arts Thesis 252, University of Hawaii, Honolulu, 1951.

Cox, J. Halley with William H. Davenport. *Hawaiian Sculpture.* Honolulu: The University Press of Hawaii, 1974.

Damon, Ethel M., ed. "The First Mission Settlement on Kauai. Being Extracts from the Manuscript Journals of Rev. Samuel Whitney and Mrs. Mercy Partridge Whitney, 1819–1824." *The Friend* 95 (1925): 204–210.

Damon, Gertrude MacKinnon. *Notebooks of Gertrude MacKinnon Damon.* N.p. Moanalua Gardens Foundation, Inc., Honolulu, n.d. Ms.

Dampier, Robert. *In the Sandwich Islands on H.M.S. Blonde.* Edited by Pauline King Joerger. Honolulu: University Press of Hawaii, 1971.

Daws, Gavan. *Shoal of Time. A History of the Hawaiian Islands.* Toronto: The Macmillan Co., 1968.

Dickey, Lyle A. "Stories of Wailua, Hawaii." *Hawaiian Historical Society*

Bibliography

Annual Report 25 (1917):14–36. Honolulu: Paradise of the Pacific Press.

Dodd, Edward. *Polynesian Art. Vol. 1. The Ring of Fire.* New York: Dodd, Mead & Company, 1967.

Edge-Partington, James, and Heape, Charles. *An Album of the Weapons, Tools, Ornaments, Articles of Dress, etc., of Natives of the Pacific Islands.* 3 vols. Manchester: J. C. Norbury, 1890–1898.

Eichhorn, August. "Alt-Hawaiische Kultobjekte und Kultgeräte." *Baessler-Archiv,* Alte Folge 13 (1929):1–30.

Elbert, Samuel H. and Mahoe, Noelani. *Nā Mele o Hawai'i Nei. 101 Hawaiian Songs.* Honolulu: University of Hawaii Press, 1970.

Emerson, Nathaniel B. *Unwritten Literature of Hawaii. The Sacred Songs of the Hula.* Bureau of American Ethnology Bulletin 38. Washington, D. C., 1909.

_____. *Pele and Hiiaka, a Myth of Hawaii.* Honolulu: Honolulu Star-Bulletin, Ltd., 1915.

Emerson, Oliver Pomeroy. *Pioneer Days in Hawaii.* Garden City, N. Y.: Doubleday, Doran & Co. Inc., 1928.

Field, Isobel. *This Life I've Loved.* New York: Longmans, Green and Co., 1937.

Forbes, A. C. "Hawaiian Tradition of the Origin of Fire." *Hawaiian Almanac and Annual for 1879,* pp. 59–60. Honolulu: Thomas G. Thrum, Pub.

Force, Roland W. and Force, Maryanne. *Art and Artifacts of the 18th Century. Objects in the Leverian Museum as Painted by Sarah Stone.* Honolulu: Bishop Museum Press, 1968.

Fornander, Abraham. *An Account of the Polynesian Race.* 3 vols. London: Trübner & Co., 1878–1885.

_____. *Fornander Collection of Hawaiian Antiquities and Folk-Lore.* Edited and translated by Thomas G. Thrum. Bernice P. Bishop Museum Memoirs IV, V, VI. Honolulu: Bishop Museum Press, 1916–1919.

Frowe, Margaret Mary S. "The History of the Theatre during the Reign of King Kalakaua, 1874–1891." Master of Arts Thesis 148. University of Hawaii, Honolulu, 1937.

Handy, E. S. C. *Polynesian Religion.* Bernice P. Bishop Museum Bulletin 34. Honolulu: The Museum, 1927.

_____. "Cultural Revolution in Hawaii." Preliminary Paper. Institute of Pacific Relations. Honolulu, 1931.

H. L. S. (Henry L. Sheldon?). "Reminiscences of Theatricals in Honolulu." *Hawaiian Almanac and Annual for 1881* 3:34–39.

Hornblow, Arthur. *A History of the Theatre in America.* 2 vols. Philadelphia: J. R. Lippincott Co., 1919.

Hoyt, Helen P. "Theatre in Hawaii (1778–1840)." *Hawaiian Historical Society Annual Report* 69 (1961):7–19.

HULA KI'I: Hawaiian Puppetry

Hutton, Laurence. *Curiosities of the American Stage.* New York: Harper & Bros., 1891.

I'i, John Papa. *Fragments of Hawaiian History.* Translated by Mary Kawena Pukui. Edited by Dorothy B. Barrère. Honolulu: Bishop Museum Press, 1959.

Judd, Laura Fish. *Honolulu. Sketches of Life in the Hawaiian Islands from 1828 to 1861.* Edited by Dale L. Morgan. Chicago: Lakeside Press, 1966.

Kaeppler, Adrienne L. "Dance and the Interpretation of Pacific Traditional Literature." In *Directions in Pacific Traditional Literature. Essays in Honor of Katharine Luomala.* Edited by Adrienne L. Kaeppler and H. Arlo Nimmo, pp. 195–216. Bernice P. Bishop Museum Special Publication 62. Honolulu: Bishop Museum Press, 1976.

_____. "*L'Aigle* and HMS *Blonde*, the Use of History in the Study of Ethnography." *The Hawaiian Journal of History* 12 (1978):28–44.

_____. "A Survey of Polynesian Art with Selected Interpretation." In *Exploring the Visual Art of Oceania.* Edited by Sydney M. Mead, pp. 180–191. Honolulu: University Press of Hawaii, 1979.

Kalakaua, His Hawaiian Majesty. *The Legends and Myths of Hawaii.* Edited with an Introduction by R. M. Daggett. New York: Charles L. Webster & Company, 1888.

Kamakau, Samuel M. *Ruling Chiefs of Hawaii.* Honolulu: Kamehameha Schools Press, 1961.

_____. *The Works of the People of Old. Na Hana a ka Po'e Kahiko.* Translated by Mary Kawena Pukui. Arr. and edited by Dorothy B. Barrère. Bernice P. Bishop Museum Special Publication 61. Honolulu: Bishop Museum Press, 1976.

Kealiinohomoku, Joann Wheeler. "A Court Dancer Disagrees with Emerson's Classic Book on the Hula." *Ethnomusicology* 8 (1964):161–164.

Koch, Gerd. "Hundert Jahre Museum für Völkerkunde Berlin Abstellung Südsee." *Baessler-Archiv.* Neue Folge 21 (1973):141-174.

Korn, Alfons L. *News from Molokai. Letters between Peter Kaeo and Queen Emma 1873–1876.* Honolulu: University Press of Hawaii, 1976.

Kotzebue, Otto von. *Entdeckungs-Reise in die Süd-See und nach der Berings-Strasse . . . 1815, 1816, 1817, und 1818. . . .* 3 vols. Weimar: Gebrüder Hoffman, 1821.

_____. *Neue Reise um die Welt, in den Jahren 1823, 24, 25, und 26.* 2 vols. in 1. Weimar: Wilhelm Hoffman, 1830.

Kuykendall, Ralph S. *The Hawaiian Kingdom 1854–1874. Twenty Critical Years.* Honolulu: University of Hawaii Press, 1953.

Luomala, Katharine. "Notes on the Development of Polynesian Hero-Cycles." *The Journal of the Polynesian Society* 49 (1940):367–374.

Bibliography

    _____. *Voices on the Wind. Polynesian Myths and Chants.* Honolulu: Bishop Museum Press, 1955.

    _____. "Moving and Movable Images in Easter Island Custom and Myth." *The Journal of the Polynesian Society* 82 (1973):28–46.

    _____. "Symbolic Slaying in Niue: Post-European Changes in a Dramatic Ritual Complex." In *The Changing Pacific. Essays in Honor of H. E. Maude.* Edited by Niel Gunson, pp. 142–162. Melbourne: Oxford University Press, 1978.

    _____. "Post-European Central Polynesian Head Masks and Puppet-Marionette Heads." *Asian Perspectives* 20 (1979):130–171.

    _____. " 'Folly & Vanity'? Native Hawaiian Puppetry." *The Puppetry Journal* 32 (1981):4–7.

    _____. "Secular, Humanoid Puppet Images in Hawaiian Oral Art." Orissa, India: Institute of Oriental and Orissan Studies, forthcoming.

Lyman, R. A. "Recollections of Kamehameha V." *Hawaiian Historical Society Annual Report* 3 (1895):12–19. Honolulu: Robert Grieve, Printer.

McAllister, J. Gilbert. *Archaeology of Oahu.* Bernice P. Bishop Museum Bulletin 104. Honolulu: The Museum, 1933.

McPharlin, Paul. *The Puppet Theater in America. A History, 1524–1948.* (With a Supplement by Marjorie Batchelder McPharlin, "Puppets in America since 1948.") Boston: Plays, Inc., 1969.

Malkin, Michael R. *Traditional and Folk Puppets of the World.* South Brunswick and New York: A. S. Barnes and Co. Inc., 1977.

    _____. "Hawaiian Puppets." In *Puppets: Art & Entertainment,* pp. 18–19. Washington, D.C.: Puppeteers of America Inc., 1980.

Malo, David. *Hawaiian Antiquities (Moolelo Hawaii).* Translated by N. B. Emerson. Edited by W. D. Alexander. 2nd ed. Bernice P. Bishop Museum Special Publication 2. Honolulu: The Museum, 1951.

Mellen, Kathleen. "Honolulu's First Lady." *Paradise of the Pacific* 63 (1952):36–38,119.

Menghin, Oswald. *Weltgeschichte der Steinzeit.* Vienna: Anton Schroll & Co., 1931.

Na Makani o Moanalua. (The Winds of Moanalua) 3(3), March, 1978.

Noble, Gurre Pioner. "Today's Guardians of Old Hulas and Hula Chants." *Paradise of the Pacific* 58 (1946):38–40.

Poignant, Roslyn. *Oceanic Mythology.* London: Paul Hamlyn, 1967.

Pollenz, Philippa. "The Puzzle of Hula." *American Anthropologist* 50 (1948):647–656.

    _____. "Changes in the Form and Function of Hawaiian Hulas." *American Anthropologist* 52 (1950):225–234.

Pukui, Mary Kawena. "Part II. Notes from a *Kumu Hula.* Selected Articles by Mary Kawena Pukui." In *Hula: Historical Perspectives.* By Dorothy B. Barrère, Mary Kawena Pukui, Marion Kelly, pp. 69–94. Bishop Museum Anthropological Records 30. Honolulu, 1980.

HULA KI'I: Hawaiian Puppetry

_____ and Curtis, Caroline. *Tales of the Menehune, and Other Short Legends of the Hawaiian Islands.* Honolulu: Kamehameha Schools Press, 1960.

_____ and Elbert, Samuel H. *Hawaiian-English Dictionary.* Honolulu: University of Hawaii Press, 1957.

_____; Elbert, Samuel H.; Mookini, Esther T. *Place Names of Hawaii.* Rev. and enl. ed. Honolulu: University Press of Hawaii, 1974.

Rice, William Hyde. *Hawaiian Legends.* Bernice P. Bishop Museum Bulletin 3. Honolulu: The Museum, 1923.

Rozina, L. G. "The James Cook Collection in the Museum of Anthropology and Ethnography Leningrad." In *Cook Voyage Artifacts in Leningrad, Berne, and Florence Museums.* Edited by Adrienne L. Kaeppler, pages 3–17. Bernice P. Bishop Museum Special Publication 66. Honolulu: Bishop Museum Press, 1978.

Ruggles, Samuel and Nancy. "From a Missionary Journal." *Atlantic Monthly* 134 (1924):648–657.

Ruschenberger, William Samuel Waithman. *A Voyage Round the World . . . in 1835, 1836, and 1837.* Philadelphia: Carey, Lea & Blanchard, 1838.

Sachs, Curt. *World History of the Dance.* Translated by Bessie Schönberg. New York: W. W. Norton & Company, Inc., 1937.

Scott, Edward B. *The Saga of the Sandwich Islands.* Lake Tahoe, Nevada: Sierra-Tahoe Publishing Co., 1968.

Speaight, George. *Punch & Judy, a History.* Boston: Plays, Inc., 1970.

Thrum, Thomas G. *Hawaiian Folk Tales.* Chicago: A. C. McClurg & Co., 1907.

_____. *More Hawaiian Folk Tales.* Chicago: A. C. McClurg & Co., 1923.

_____. "Legend of Pupu-hulu-ana." *The Hawaiian Annual for 1926* (1925):92–95.

Thurston, Lorrin Andrews. *Memoirs of the Hawaiian Revolution.* Edited by Andrew Farrell. Honolulu: Advertiser Publishing Co., Ltd., 1936.

Westervelt, W. D. *Legends of Ma-ui—A Demi God of Polynesia, and of His Mother Hina.* Honolulu: The Hawaiian Gazette Co., Ltd., 1910.

_____. *Legends of Old Honolulu.* George H. Ellis Co., Boston, 1925.

Withington, Antoinette. *Hawaiian Tapestry.* New York: Harper & Brothers, 1937.

Wood, John George. *The Natural History of Man; Being an Account of the Manners and Customs of the Uncivilized Races of Men.* 2 vols. London: George Routledge and Sons, 1868–1880. (Also, Wood, John George. *The Uncivilized Races of Men in All the Countries of the World.* 2 vols. in 1. Hartford: The J. B. Burr Publishing Co., 1877.)

INDEX

Aberrant images, 51–3
Ahu'ena Heiau, 6, 16, 77, 134
Alexander, William DeWitt, 121, 125
American Ethnology, U.S. Bureau of, 25–6
Animals, images of, 15, 60, 143
Arning, Doctor Eduard, 55, 56, 64
Auld, William, 125

Bacon, Patience Wiggin, 131
Barrère, Dorothy, 74
Barrot, Theodore-Adolphe, 91
Beamer, Helen Desha, 135
Beamer, Joanne, 136
Beamer, Winona, 15, 40, 123, 127, 135, 136
Beattie, James, 2, 91
Beckwith, Martha Warren, 146
Berlin Museum feather image, 24–5, 59
Berlin Museum head, 35, 64–7
Berlin Museum torso, 55–8
Bingham, Reverend Hiram A., 74, 120, 129
Birds, images of, 15, 16
Bishop, Princess Bernice Pauahi, 34
Bishop Museum "doll," 51–2
Bishop Museum "puppet," 52–3
Bishop Museum puppets, 16, 17, 20, 57, 65; description, 24–5, 37–8; history, 33–6, 40–1
Blonde (ship), 3, 10, 11, 61, 63, 91–2
Bloxam, Andrew, 61–2, 63
Bloxam, Andrew Roby, 62
Bloxam, Matthew Holbeche, 62
Bloxam, Reverend Richard Rouse, 62
Bloxam, Reverend Richard Rowland, 61, 63
Brigham, William T., 22
British Museum Ethnographical Handbook, 23
British Museum heads, 16, 17, 55, 58–64
British Museum puppet, 55, 59, 65; description, 17–21; function, 21–4
Bryan, William Alanson, 34, 90, 99
Buck, Peter H., 9, 19, 60, 65
Burns, Eugene, 135
Byron, Lord George Anson, 3, 4

HULA KI'I: Hawaiian Puppetry

California, 4, 134, 171
Campbell, Archibald, 2
Castle, William R., 125
Charlot, Jean, 23–4
Chiefs, images of, 18, 21–4, 28–9; and *mahiole* (helmet) style, 27–8, 62
Choris, Louis, 6, 7, 73
Cook, Captain James, 2, 58, 63, 170
Costa, Mazeppa King, 75, 76
Cox, J. Halley, 5–6, 9, 22, 55–6, 60, 63

Damon, Gerturde MacKinnon, 34–5, 38, 39, 73, 90, 97, 99, 100
Damon, Samuel M., 34
Dampier, Robert, 10–11
Dancers, 99; and puppet actors, 136–38; and puppets as body masks, 135–36; with or without sacred images, 131–34; without puppets, 117–31
Davenport, William H., 5–6, 9, 22, 55–6, 60, 63
Davis, Isaac, 2
Deaves, Walter E., 39, 89–90
Derby, Charles, 4
Desha, Isabella Kaili, 135–36
Dixon, George, 58
Dodd, Edward, 23
Drama, development of, 91–7

Edge-Partington, James, 23
Eel-man, 66–7
Elbert, Samuel H., 30, 127–28
Ellis, Reverend William, 63
Emerson, Nathaniel B., 79, 80, 117, 121–31 *passim;* on functions of puppets, 71, 72, 73, 75, 76; on human participation, 97, 98, 101; on puppet plays, 91, 92, 93, 95, 96, 97; on six royal Hawaiian puppets, 1, 25–39 *passim*
Emerson, Reverend Oliver P., 40–1, 72, 77, 121–22
Emma, Queen, 137

Foreign troupes, influence of, 2, 4, 87–91, 137–38, 170–71
  See also Punch and Judy shows, influence of
Fornander, Abraham, 119
Franks, August W., 17
Function of puppets: as entertainment, 71–2, 171–72; and religious significance, debate over, 73–8

Gomes, Keahi Luahine Sylvester, 131, 132
Greenwell, Amy, 52–3
Grieve, Robert, 125

Index

Halemano, Chief, 15, 144–46
Hale-o-Keawe mausoleum, 63, 64
Haleole, S. M., 94
Haumea (goddess), 56–7
Hawai'i, island of, 134, 141, 171
Head images, 55, 58–67, 74
Heape, Charles, 23
Heiaus, 16, 73, 74, 75. See also 'Ahu'ena Heiau
Hewahewa, 77
Hi'iaka (goddess), 84, 101–02, 133, 166
Hi'ilani (puppet), 35–7
Hoamakeikekula, 166–67
Ho'āo (marriage ceremony), 128, 130
Holokū (dress), 30
Honolulu Opera House, 81, 86, 87, 88, 92, 170
Ho'oleheleheki'i, 96–97
Ho'opa'apa'a contest, 143–144
Huhu, Kini Kapahukula-o-Kamamalu. See Wilson, Jenny
Hui, 35
Hula schools *(hula hālau)*, 73–5, 80, 81
Human participants, 97–9
Hungry Child, The (mele), 100

I'i, John Papa, 119
Images, varieties, 5–11, 79, 170–72; sacred *(kapu)*, 5, 10, 15, 73, 74, 78; secular *(noa)*, 5–10, 77–8
Instruments *(hula ki'i)*, 81–2, 85, 87
Iolani Palace, 123

Ka'ahumanu, Queen, 8, 64
Kaeppler, Adrienne L., 9–10, 63, 126
Kahunas, 8, 16
Kaikio'ewa, 129–30
Kaipalaoa, 143–44
Ka'iulani, Princess, 88
Kala'imamahu, 64
Kālaipāhoa (god), 56
Kalākaua, King David, 27, 40, 41, 57, 64, 81, 92, 136–37, 150, 170; birthday celebration, 26, 81, 86, 87, 90; coronation, 83–4, 90, 122–26, 134, 171; wedding night, 135
Kalama, Queen, 26
Kalanimoku, 4, 63, 97
Kalani'ōpu'u, King, 118–19, 120
Kaloakea, 2
Kalukuna, 2
Kamaikui, Grace. See Kalukuna
Kamakau, Samuel M., 6, 117–21, 130, 134

HULA KI'I: Hawaiian Puppetry

Kamalālāwalu, King, 95, 96
Kamāmalu, Queen, 3, 120
Kamapua'a, 15
Kāmeha'ikana (goddess), 56, 57–8
Kamehameha I, King. See Kamehameha the Great, King
Kamehameha II, King, 3, 6, 7, 26, 64, 81, 119–20
Kamehameha III, King, 26, 27, 91, 92, 129–30
Kamehameha IV, King, 27, 129
Kamehameha V, 27, 40, 129
Kamehameha the Great, King, 2, 6, 22, 23, 56, 57, 64, 86, 97, 102, 164–65
Kaneopa, 165–66
Kapihe, 129
Kapi'olani, Queen, 84, 135
Kapuaiwa, Lot. See Kamehameha V, King
Kapule, Queen, 1, 8, 85
Kaua'i, 1, 85, 101, 132–34, 141, 171
Kauakāhiakawa'ū, Chief, 146–48
Kauikeaoūli. See Kamehameha III, King
Kau'ilani, 163
Kaumuali'i, King, 1, 7, 26, 32, 85, 134
Kawehiokanāhele (puppet), 35–7, 101
Kawelo, Chief, 95, 164
Keana, Chiefess, 120
Kekauluohi, Chiefess, 64
Kekuaiwa, Prince Moses, 130
Keohonina, Ehu, 123, 124, 125
Ke'ōpūolani, Queen, 102, 129
Kepelino, 117–18
Kewelani, 101
Kihawahine (goddess), 57
Ki'iki'i (puppet), 28, 96–97
Kilu betting game, 101
Kini Ki'i (puppet), 26, 28, 29, 31, 96, 97
Kōleamoku (god), 16
Konikonia, Chief, 148–50
Kotzebue, Otto von, 3–4, 21
Ku (puppet), 96, 97
Kū (god), 22, 97
Kuakini, Chief, 97
Kūkā'ilimoku (god), 22
Kukuhoi, 64
Kumulipo, (creation chant), 150, 151, 152

Leleihoku, Chief William Pitt, 129
Leningrad Museum, 18

Index

Lever, Sir Ashton, 58
Leverian Museum, London, 58
Liholiho. *See* Kamehameha II, King
Liholiho, Alexander. *See* Kamehameha IV, King
Likelike, Princess, 88
Liliuokalani, Queen, 88, 89, 150
Loh'iau, 84, 101–02, 133
Lono (god), 6, 15, 16, 76, 143
Luahine, Iolani, 131, 132–33, 134
Lunalilo, King William C., 136, 137

McAllister, J. Gilbert, 66
Maccabe, 88
McDonald's restaurants, 38
McDonough, John E., 89
McPharlin, Paul, 89
Mailelauli'i (puppet), 29–32, 92–96
Mailepākaha (puppet), 26, 29–32, 92–96
Makahiki celebration, 22, 76
Makakūikalani (puppet), 28–32, 92–96
Mākālei (puppet), 35–7, 100–01
Malkin, Michael R., 25
Malo, David, 121
Manini, John, 66
Maui, 152
Meles (action songs), 71–2, 126–34; and Kalākaua's coronation, 122–26; translations of, 98–102, 118–19, 126–31, 132
Menghin, Oswald, 75
Millis, Fred W., 87, 88–9
Missionary opposition, 8, 87, 117, 120–22, 124–25, 170
Moanalua, 34, 35, 40, 99
Munich Ethnological Museum, 7
Musée de l'Homme, Paris, 23
Music Hall. *See* Honolulu Opera House
Mu'umu'u (dress), 30

Nahainaka, 33–4, 38
Nāhi'ena'ena, Princess, 102, 129
Namakahelu, 99
Narratives, and puppet themes, 141–153, 163–67, 171–72
National Museum of Natural History, Smithsonian Institution, puppets, 16, 17, 19, 20, 24, 36, 37, 41, 65–6; description, 27–3; history, 25–7, 92
Nihiaumoe (puppet), 28–31, 96
Noble, Gurre Pioner, 133

HULA KI'I: Hawaiian Puppetry

O'ahu, 41, 134, 141, 171
Origins of Hawaiian puppets, 73–76, 85, 117, 134, 170; and foreign influence, 2–4. *See also* Punch and Judy shows, influence of
"Oscar and Malvina" drama, 2, 91

Pa'akaula, 33, 34, 35, 36, 38, 40, 64, 74, 90, 100
Paaluhi, 37, 38
Pacific Commercial Advertiser, 39, 86, 88
Papa. *See* Haumea
Pele (goddess), 23, 84, 101, 133–34
Performances, 80–3; programming for, 83–4
Perry, Kaoanaeha, 66
Pflüger, J. W., 64
Pi'imaiwa'a, 164–65
Poignant, Roslyn, 23
Polynesian art, categories of, 9–10, 33, 41, 52, 53, 61, 62, 66
Polynesian culture, and dance, 75–7
Portlock, Nathaniel, 58
Potomac (frigate), 92
Prince Lot Hula Festival, 40, 136
Pua'akukui (purification ceremony), 15–6
Puapuakea (puppet), 28–33, 92–96
Pukui, Mary Kawena, 30, 37–8, 132, 133
Punch and Judy shows, influence of, 37, 38–41, 86, 97, 100–01, 136, 171
Puppeteers, 8, ;79–80, 81, 93
Puppet mimicry, 82–3
Pupuakea. *See* Puapuakea
Pūpūhulu'ana, 163

Randell, E., 17
Revolution of 1819, 63, 73, 77, 78
Rice, Thomas D., 137
Royal Hawaiian Theatre, 89
Rugby School Museum, Warwickshire, England, 62
Ruggles, Nancy, 85–6
Ruggles, Samuel, 85
Ruschenberger, William Samuel Waithman, 11

Sachs, Curt, 75, 76
Screen, use of, 79, 81, 85, 86–7
Stone, Sarah, 58, 60
Structural types of puppets, 16–7, 33, 40, 169–70

Tapa, use of, 17–8, 19, 25, 29, 30, 59, 60, 79, 80, 85
Temple Square Museum, Salt Lake City, 23
Torso. *See* Berlin Museum torso

Index

von Kotzebue, Otto. *See* Kotzebue, Otto von

Wākea, 150–52
Whitney, Samuel, 85
Williams, J. J., 20–1
Wilson, Jenny, 39–40, 123, 127
Wood, Reverend J. G., 17, 18, 19–20, 21